from Ryan
Christmas 2002

D1271773

BIG BLUE

100 Years of Kentucky Wildcats Basketball

by Michael Bradley

The SportingNews

Photo Credits

Back cover photo: Brian Spurlock. **4-5:** Brian Spurlock. **6-7:** The Sporting News Archives. **8-9:** (clockwise from left) Brian Spurlock; Brian Spurlock; Brian Spurlock; Brian Spurlock; David Coyle; Brian Spurlock; AP/Wide World Photos; Brian Spurlock. **10:** (inset) Brian Spurlock; Brian Spurlock. **12:** Brian Spurlock. **13:** Malcolm Emmons. **14:** top, Brian Spurlock; bottom, Brian Spurlock. **15:** David Coyle. **16:** AP/Wide World Photos. **17:** Brian Spurlock. **18-19:** (clockwise from left) David Coyle; AP/Wide World Photos; AP/Wide World Photos; Bob Leverone/The Sporting News; AP/Wide World Photos; Malcolm Emmons; Brian Spurlock. **20-21:** (inset) David Coyle; AP/Wide World Photos. **22-23:** (inset) The Sporting News Archives; AP/Wide World Photos. **24-25:** (inset) David Coyle; AP/Wide World Photos. **26-27:** (inset) David Coyle, AP/Wide World Photos. **28-29:** (inset) David Coyle, Malcolm Emmons. **30-31:** (inset) David Coyle, Brian Spurlock. **32-33:** (inset) David Coyle; Bob Leverone/The Sporting News. **34-35:** AP/Wide World Photos. **36-37:** (inset) Brian Spurlock; Brian Spurlock. **38-39:** Brian Spurlock. **40-41:** (clockwise from left) Rich Clarkson and Associates; AP/Wide World Photos; Rich Clarkson and Associates; Rich Clarkson and Associates; Malcolm Emmons; Bob Leverone/The Sporting News; The Sporting News Archives; The Sporting News Archives; The Sporting News Archives; Brian Spurlock. **42:** Malcolm Emmons. **43:** top, AP/Wide World Photos; bottom, AP/Wide World Photos. **44-45:** Rich Clarkson and Associates. **46:** Rich Clarkson and Associates. **47:** top, Malcolm Emmons; bottom left, Rich Clarkson and Associates; bottom right, Rich Clarkson and Associates. **48:** Malcolm Emmons. **49:** top, The Sporting News Archives; bottom left, Malcolm Emmons; bottom right, The Sporting News Archives. **50:** The Sporting News Archives. **51:** top, The Sporting News Archives; bottom left, Brian Spurlock; bottom right, Brian Spurlock. **52:** Bob Leverone/The Sporting News. **53:** top, Albert Dickson/The Sporting News; bottom left, The Sporting News Archives; bottom right, David Coyle. **54-55:** (clockwise from left) AP/Wide World Photos; Malcolm Emmons; Brian Spurlock; Rich Clarkson and Associates; Malcolm Emmons; The Sporting News Archives. **56:** Rich Clarkson and Associates. **57:** Malcolm Emmons. **58:** Rich Clarkson and Associates. **59:** AP/Wide World Photos. **60:** AP/Wide World Photos. **61:** AP/Wide World Photos. **62:** (inset) Brian Spurlock; The Sporting News Archives. **63:** The Sporting News Archives. **64:** The Sporting News Archives. **65:** The Sporting News Archives. **66:** The Sporting News Archives. **67:** Rich Clarkson and Associates. **68:** AP/Wide World Photos. **69:** The Sporting News Archives. **70:** AP/Wide World Photos. **71:** Malcolm Emmons. **72:** The Sporting News Archives. **73:** Malcolm Emmons. **74:** Rich Clarkson and Associates. **75:** AP/Wide World Photos. **76:** top, AP/Wide World Photos; (inset), Rich Clarkson and Associates; bottom, AP/Wide World Photos. **77:** (clockwise from left) Brian Spurlock; Brian Spurlock; Brian Spurlock; Rich Clarkson and Associates; David Coyle; Dilip Vishwanat/The Sporting News Archives; Rich Clarkson and Associates; The Courier-Journal. **78-79:** (clockwise from left) David Coyle; The Sporting News Archives; Rich Clarkson and Associates; The Courier-Journal; Dilip Vishwanat/The Sporting News; Rich Clarkson and Associates; AP/Wide World Photos. **80:** top, The Courier-Journal; center, The Courier-Journal; bottom, The Courier-Journal. **81:** The Courier-Journal. **82:** top, The Courier-Journal; bottom, The Courier-Journal. **83:** The Courier-Journal. **84:** top, David Coyle; bottom, Malcolm Emmons. **85:** left, AP/Wide World Photos; right, AP/Wide World Photos. **86:** Rich Clarkson and Associates. **87:** The Sporting News Archives. **88:** Malcolm Emmons. **89:** Malcolm Emmons. **90:** Malcolm Emmons. **91:** Rich Clarkson and Associates. **92:** Rich Clarkson and Associates. **93:** Malcolm Emmons. **94:** left, Malcolm Emmons; right, AP/Wide World Photos. **95:** Malcolm Emmons. **96:** The Courier-Journal. **97:** left, Brian Spurlock; right, Brian Spurlock. **98:** Rich Clarkson and Associates. **99:** The Sporting News Archives. **100:** AP/Wide World Photos. **101:** Rich Clarkson and Associates. **102:** Rich Clarkson and Associates. **103:** left, Dilip Vishwanat/The Sporting News; right, The Sporting News Archives. **104:** top, Malcolm Emmons; bottom, The Sporting News Archives. **105:** left, Brian Spurlock; right, Brian Spurlock. **106:** left, David Coyle; right, Malcolm Emmons. **107:** The Sporting News Archives. **108:** top left, Brian Spurlock; bottom left, Malcolm Emmons; right, The Courier-Journal. **109:** left, Dilip Vishwanat/The Sporting News; right, The Courier-Journal. **110:** top, Brian Spurlock; bottom, Rich Clarkson and Associates. **111:** left, The Sporting News Archives; right, The Sporting News Archives. **112:** Brian Spurlock. **113:** left, Rich Clarkson and Associates; right, AP/Wide World Photos. **114:** left, Brian Spurlock; right, Malcolm Emmons. **115:** Brian Spurlock. **116:** (left to right) Brian Spurlock David Coyle; Lexington Herald-Leader; Lexington Herald-Leader; Brian Spurlock; David Coyle. **118:** Lexington Herald-Leader. **120:** Lexington Herald-Leader. **122:** Brian Spurlock. **124:** (inset) The Courier-Journal; David Coyle. **126-127:** (clockwise from left) AP/Wide World Photos; AP/Wide World Photos; The Sporting News Archives; The Sporting News Archives; David Coyle; AP/Wide World Photos; AP/Wide World Photos. **128:** AP/Wide World Photos. **129:** AP/Wide World Photos. **130:** (inset) AP/Wide World Photos; AP/Wide World Photos. **132:** (inset) AP/Wide World Photos; AP/Wide World Photos. **133:** AP/Wide World Photos. **134:** AP/Wide World Photos. **135:** AP/Wide World Photos; (inset) AP/Wide World Photos. **136-137:** Steve Franz. **138:** David Coyle. **139:** David Coyle. **140:** (inset) David Coyle; David Coyle. **142:** AP/Wide World Photos. **143:** AP/Wide World Photos. **144:** (inset) AP/Wide World Photos; AP/Wide World Photos. **146:** The Courier-Journal. **147:** AP/Wide World Photos. **148-149:** (clockwise from bottom left) David Coyle; AP/Wide World Photos: David Coyle; AP/Wide World Photos; AP/Wide World Photos; AP/Wide World Photos; AP/Wide World Photos. **150:** AP/Wide World Photos. **151:** AP/Wide World Photos. **152:** AP/Wide World Photos. **154:** Bettmann/CORBIS. **156:** AP/Wide World Photos. **158:** AP/Wide World Photos. **159:** AP/Wide World Photos. **160:** David Coyle. **161:** David Coyle. **162:** AP/Wide World Photos. **163:** AP/Wide World Photos. **164:** The Courier-Journal. **165:** The Courier-Journal. **166:** AP/Wide World Photos. **167:** (inset) AP/Wide World Photos. **168:** AP/Wide World Photos. **169:** AP/Wide World Photos. **170:** (clockwise from left); AP/Wide World Photos; The Courier-Journal; David Coyle; AP/Wide World Photos; AP/Wide World Photos; Dilip Vishwanat/The Sporting News; center, The Sporting News Archives; Rich Clarkson and Associates; David Coyle. **174:** The Sporting News Archives. **175:** The Sporting News Archives. **176:** top, AP/Wide World Photos; bottom, AP/Wide World Photos. **177:** left, AP/Wide World Photos; bottom, AP/Wide World Photos; right, The Courier-Journal. **178:** Malcolm Emmons. **179:** Malcolm Emmons. **180:** left, AP/Wide World Photos; right, The Courier-Journal. **181:** top, Malcolm Emmons; bottom, AP/Wide World Photos. **182:** AP/Wide World Photos. **183:** Rich Clarkson and Associates. **184:** left, Malcolm Emmons; right, Malcolm Emmons. **185:** top, AP/Wide World Photos; bottom, The Sporting News Archives. **186:** left, The Sporting News Archives; right, David Coyle. **187:** AP/Wide World Photos. **188:** David Coyle. **189:** Dilip Vishwanat/The Sporting News.

Copyright © 2002 by The Sporting News, a division of Vulcan Sports Media, 10176 Corporate Square Drive, Suite 200, St. Louis MO 63132. All rights reserved.

No part of *Big Blue: 100 Years of Kentucky Wildcats Basketball* may be reproduced or transmitted in any form or by any means, electronic or mechanical, including photocopy, recording or any other information storage and retrieval system now known or to be invented, without permission in writing from the publisher, except by a reviewer who wishes to quote brief passages in connection with a review written for inclusion in a magazine, newspaper or broadcast.

The Sporting News is a federally registered trademark of Vulcan Sports Media, Inc. Visit our website at www.sportingnews.com.

ISBN: 0-89204-691-0

Acknowledgements

Capturing 100 years of University of Kentucky basketball was a daunting task right from the opening tipoff. But the staff of *The Sporting News*, pulling together in the same manner that Wildcats teams have done throughout the storied history of the UK program, got the job done with the efficiency of a Dan Issel power move to the basket.

Teamwork has been crucial at Alumni Gym, Memorial Coliseum and Rupp Arena over the years, and it has been just as important in the offices of *The Sporting News*. Without it, UK would never have achieved greatness on the court and TSN would never have stepped to the forefront in sports-book publishing.

I'd like to thank those whose dedication to *Big Blue: 100 Years of Kentucky Wildcats Basketball* can best be described as a total team effort. Free-lance writer Michael Bradley and TSN senior editor Joe Hoppel were the key editorial forces behind this project. Barry Reeves, who attended the University of Kentucky and is another of TSN's own, provided invaluable assistance as a consultant and also wrote the text for the book's first chapter, "Basketball in the Bluegrass State." Barry never admitted it, but I suspect he had Kyle Macy and Jack Givens posters hanging in his bedroom while growing up in Mayfield, Ky.

Reeves also oversaw the balloting that determined UK's all-time first, second and third teams and the voting that ranked the greatest performances and the most exciting moments in Wildcats history. He put together a voting panel made up of lead writer Bradley; TSN's Hoppel, Reeves, Dave Kindred, Mike DeCourcy, Matt Hayes and longtime correspondent Mike Strange; Kentucky media members Rick Bozich, Rob Bromley, John Clay, Pat Forde, Ralph Hacker, Tom Leach, Billy Reed, Mark Story, Jerry Tipton and Larry Vaught; and former Wildcats Winston Bennett, Larry Conley, Louie Dampier, Jack Givens, Cliff Hagan, Bill Keightley (equipment manager), Kyle Macy, Cotton Nash, C.M. Newton (a former UK athletic director and player) and Kenny Walker. TSN is grateful for the time and effort that these voters devoted to this endeavor.

The book's design was created by Pamela Speh, with special input from prepress director Bob Parajon. Pamela (who also did much of the prepress work) and Christen Sager designed most of the pages, with the help of Russ Carr and Michael Behrens. They were ably assisted by prepress specialists Steve Romer, Vern Kasal and Dave Brickey.

The result, I think, is a definitive book on University of Kentucky basketball. Sure, there will be debate over the rankings of greatest performances and most exciting moments in UK history. Even the voters themselves seemed conflicted. And it wasn't any easier to pick the All-UK teams, either. (One notation should be made here: The Most Exciting Moments chapter was originally called The Greatest Moments, and many voters put the hiring of Adolph Rupp—unquestionably the greatest figure in UK basketball history—at the top of their lists. Upon reflection, "Most Exciting" seemed the better title for what we were trying to convey—and that, specifically, was a look back at the most unforgettable, edge-of-the-seat moments in UK history. So, the Baron, virtually unknown at the time of his hiring, was eased out of the "Moments" category. Rest assured, though, Rupp is dominant within these pages.)

This book is aimed at all college basketball fans who have a deep appreciation of excellence, tradition and history. For those who bleed blue, excellence, tradition and history mean only one thing: Kentucky Wildcats basketball.

Steve Meyerhoff
Editorial Director

The **Sporting News**

presents

BIG BLUE

Contents

Basketball in the Bluegrass State

Basketball in the Bluegrass State

"Kentucky basketball is life."

> *—actress Ashley Judd, a onetime University of Kentucky student*

Although Judd's pronouncement may seem wildly overstated outside the Commonwealth of Kentucky, it is viewed as a simple statement of fact within the state's borders. Make no mistake, University of Kentucky basketball permeates every aspect of daily life for most of the state's four million-plus residents.

Wherever Kentuckians are and whatever they might be doing, Wildcats basketball never is far from their minds. Will the heralded point guard have the right stuff to run the team? Will the power forward recover from that nagging knee injury? Will the center apply himself in the classroom and stay eligible? Who is being recruited? What do the new uniforms look like? Who will be the backup shooting guard? Are the new seats at Rupp Arena the right shade of blue? What do those former UK coaches at Louisville and Florida have up their sleeves? Have you seen that 10th-grade forward from Ashland play? How about the freshman high schooler in Paducah with the velvet shooting touch?

In Kentucky, it's all basketball. All the time. And now, as the Wildcats embark on their 100th season of intercollegiate competition, it's a perfect time to reflect on everything that seems to make UK basketball the preeminent program in the nation.

*   *   *   *   *

"Going to Kentucky was a dream of mine."

> *—Richie Farmer, a member of UK's 1991-1992 Unforgettables*

When Farmer drew his first breath on August 25, 1969, in the hollows of the Appalachian Mountains, his destiny was a long way from being determined. But his dream, his ultimate goal, was infinitely closer.

Farmer is as Kentucky as they come. He grew up in the coal-mining town of Manchester, Ky., where the exploits of local high school basketball players instill an immeasurable sense of pride in the citizenry. Farmer was brought up on the tales of Dan Issel, Wah Wah Jones, Jimmy Dan Conner, Ralph Beard and Louie Dampier. He was told again and again of Beard's free throw that won the 1946 NIT at Madison Square Garden and thrust UK basketball into national prominence; of Vernon Hatton's 47-foot, game-tying heave in overtime against Temple in the first week of the 1957-58 season; of Issel's 51-point answer to the 64 points scored by LSU's Pete Maravich in a February 1970 shootout; of

Kentucky players—native sons, like Richie Farmer (inset) and Derek Anderson (right), or adopted, white or black—are on a pedestal.

the athletic grace and potential of 7-2 Tom Payne, Adolph Rupp's first black player. All those stories—none of which needed to be embellished—served as glittering background material as Farmer watched Kyle Macy, Jack Givens and Sam Bowie make history of their own. As a child, Richie certainly followed Macy's lead and wiped his hands on his socks before attempting free throws.

After all, Richie Farmer was born to be a Kentucky Wildcat.

* * * * *

"I fell in love with the game right away."
—*Cliff Hagan, a two-time consensus All-American at Kentucky*

Hagan grew up alongside the Ohio River in Owensboro, Ky., in the 1930s and '40s, just as basketball was exploding in popularity. He doesn't recall seeing a basketball goal before he was in the fourth grade, but it was love at first sight. Pretty soon, he and a basketball were inseparable, and before long Hagan was dominating games at the YMCA with a hook shot that truly was unstoppable.

Hagan's basketball awareness coincided with the Wildcats' emergence on the national stage and the mounting statewide frenzy and inestimable pride surrounding UK's

success. Radio coverage and newsreel film chronicled the feats of Beard, Alex Groza and the rest of the "Fabulous Five," the remarkable group that powered Kentucky to its first NCAA championship in 1948 and also helped cart home Olympic gold for the United States that summer. Hagan listened and watched as the UK legend grew—the Wildcats repeated as national champions in 1949—and he yearned to wear the white and blue.

Cliff Hagan was born to be a Kentucky Wildcat.

* * * * *

"When a Kentucky baby is born, his mother naturally wants him to be President, like another Kentuckian, Abraham Lincoln. If not President, she wants him to play basketball for the University of Kentucky."
—*Adolph Rupp, the fabled Baron of the Bluegrass, UK's coach for 41 seasons*

Some basketball-crazed fans no doubt contend that Rupp had it wrong—that, in fact, most mothers naturally want their sons to play the roundball sport for UK. Failing that, the Presidency would be a worthy second option.

No matter. The fact is, practically every Kentucky-born boy—unless born inside the Louisville city limits—dreams of becoming a Kentucky Wildcat. When a baby boy is born,

parents, grandparents, uncles, aunts and neighbors alike race to the local Wal-Mart or the Kennedy Bookstore in Lexington, jockeying to be the first to purchase that UK sleeper. Or that blue-and-white miniature basketball. Or those tiny tennis shoes with the UK logo. Or that baby bottle with the roaring wildcat. Anything that might help the dream come true for the little guy—the dream of playing basketball for the Kentucky Wildcats.

Of course, few boys actually realize this goal, yet the dream is what galvanizes the program and the state. It unifies fans and players. It is the common thread in the fabric of Big Blue Nation.

Within reach or not, boys throughout Kentucky chase the dream—From Nerf hoop to the 6-foot goal in the basement, from the driveway to the junior high gym and then to the 5,000-seat high school arena. Kentucky boys don't imagine they are Larry Bird or Kobe Bryant or Shaquille O'Neal. They dribble around pretending to be Rex Chapman or Jamal Mashburn or Tayshaun Prince.

As the boys grow older and their shortcomings in athletic ability and skill level grow noticeable, the dream fades for many. But the emotional tie to UK basketball never wanes— even when the young men realize that God didn't bless them with the leaping ability, jump shot or height to reach Rupp Arena. Their rooms remain blue and white. The UK posters stay on the wall. And the Wildcat wardrobe grows along with the body.

Once a Wildcat fan, always a Wildcat fan.

* * * * *

"I live and die with them."
—*NASCAR legend Darrell Waltrip*

Waltrip, like Hagan, grew up in Owensboro, dreaming of wearing the blue and white, taking instruction from Adolph Rupp and having Cawood Ledford describe his every move on the basketball court. There was only one problem with Waltrip's plan to follow in the footsteps of Hagan, 15 years his senior. "I wasn't very good," Waltrip says.

So, Waltrip switched gears and jumped into a race car. For all the fame and fortune he has received because of his driving skills, it wouldn't surprise anyone if Waltrip would trade it all for a shot at wearing a Wildcats uniform.

And why not? The only difference between Hagan's dream and Waltrip's is that one came true and the other didn't.

* * * * *

"There's nothing else in the people's lives bigger than Kentucky basketball. Vacations, social life ... everything they

Kentucky's wildly supportive fans come dressed for the occasion, whether at Wildcats games or outside of Rupp Arena.

For some boys, chasing the dream of playing for the Wildcats begins with a Nerf hoop and ends with the ecstasy of winning a title while wearing a Kentucky uniform. For others, the dream falls far short—but, clearly, the emotional ties to UK basketball live on.

do with their family revolves around Kentucky basketball."

—*Rick Pitino, coach of Kentucky's 1996 NCAA championship team*

As everyone knows, Pitino has a flair for exaggeration, but he's not far off the mark here. Kentucky basketball *is* the centerpiece of the Commonwealth. It brings unanimity to a diverse population. From coal miners to crop dusters to tire makers to world-class doctors to bourbon distillers to horse trainers to teachers, Kentuckians share a love for UK basketball.

They love it so much that they've been known to ...

■ Change their wedding day so it won't conflict with a big Cats game.

■ Talk UK basketball when they're at work. At home. At church. At the grocery store. When they're in groups. Even when they're alone.

■ Shun anyone who speaks ill of their Wildcats.

■ Arrange for burial in UK-logo-emblazoned caskets.

■ Delay the delivery of children so they can watch the final minutes of a UK game on television.

■ Take delight in pep rallies—rallies beamed live on TV, believe it or not.

■ Burn vacation days so they can arrive at Memorial Coliseum weeks before practice begins each October to have the honor of being among the first to see the new edition of the Cats.

■ Lobby TV and radio stations in a dozen states to broadcast Wildcats games. Transplanted Kentuckians need their fix—and they get it. UK games are carried on about 100 radio stations overall, a dozen TV stations and two regional cable networks.

■ Travel near and far to see their Wildcats play. So much so that the Georgia Dome in Atlanta is referred to as "Rupp Arena South." One Cats fan actually attended 700 consecutive games, home and away, at venues that included Japan, Hawaii, Alaska and Puerto Rico.

■ Settle divorces only when the parties involved agree to share season tickets.

■ Skip the Academy Awards ceremony for an important UK game—as Ashley Judd has done.

Kentuckians have their game-day rituals, too. Oh, do they. They've been known to ...

■ Wear the same articles of UK clothing to games. And different outfits for home and away games.

■ Strip down to their underwear—if they think it'll help the dear ol' blue and white.

■ Light candles—sometimes dozens of them—at the foot of homemade "altars."

■ Gather in groups—the same location, the same people, the same assigned seats—to watch the Cats on TV.

■ Watch the games in solitude, too.

■ Chant "Blue" and "White" during every timeout.
■ Wear Kentucky-blue sports coats to church every Sunday in March. That includes the preacher.
■ Name their children after UK All-Americans.
■ Close their eyes when the other team takes important shots. And when the Cats take important shots.
■ Hide behind the couch during tense moments.
■ Pace around the coffee table.
■ Have voodoo dolls ready if needed.
■ Guzzle shots of Kentucky bourbon when the team is doing poorly. Or when the team is doing well.

*   *   *   *   *

"I could try to describe (basketball's) importance here, but no one would believe it."
—*Joe B. Hall, who grew up in Cynthiana,*

Ky., played briefly at UK and succeeded Adolph Rupp as Kentucky coach

It's not just around UK basketball that this state revolves. High school basketball is a solid No. 2 on the priority list, ranking even higher than horse racing on most Kentuckians' social calendars.

Actually, it's hard to say whether UK basketball launched the high school sport upward or vice versa. Doesn't matter, really. The two are forever intertwined.

Kentucky high schools have been the lifeblood of UK's, Louisville's and Western Kentucky's national programs. Sure, most—if not all—of those schools' great teams featured out-of-state talent, but the foundation for those teams was laid in gyms in the Appalachian Mountains, atop the rolling hills of horse country, alongside the Ohio River and in the

Cats fans have been known to cheer on their team until they're blue in the face—and some of the team's more creative supporters take it a few steps further. Being born to be a Wildcats fan comes with the territory in Kentucky, where basketball—be it the UK program or high school ball—seems to permeate daily life.

Jackson Purchase lake areas.

Kentucky is the only state that still plays a one-classification, all-comers tournament—it culminates with the Sweet Sixteen—to determine its high school champion. The Kentucky state tourney might well have been the original March Madness. The journey begins with 64 district tournaments involving all schools statewide, each tourney being played before overflow crowds. The district champions and runner-up teams advance to 16 equally jam-packed regional tournaments.

The teams scratch and claw to reach the Sweet Sixteen, a cherished accomplishment because it means a trip to the Promised Land—Rupp Arena. Even if these players aren't UK material, they'll still dress in UK's locker rooms, play meaningful games on the Wildcats' floor and hear the roar of 23,000 fans. This is where city meets country, David meets Goliath. This is the stage where tiny schools like Carr Creek, Inez and Cuba go face to face, chest to chest with mega-schools from Louisville, Lexington and the Cincinnati suburbs.

The Sweet Sixteen always has been the crossroads for Kentuckians, sort of a four-day revival for the basketball faithful. The fans flock to Lexington, or sometimes Louisville's Freedom Hall, to root for the hometown team or just to savor the special wonders of their favorite sport. To cheer for tiny Carr Creek in 1928, before sending the boys off to fight for the "national championship" in Chicago. To witness the artful dribbling of Cuba's Howard Crittenden, Joe Fulks' floating jump shot, King Kelly Coleman's scoring feats, Cliff Hagan's marvelous hook shot, Wes Unseld's hulk, the Richie Farmer-Allan Houston showdown.

The most storied moment in the convergence of UK basketball and Kentucky high school ball occurred on March 16, 1957. In a defining example of Kentuckians' passion for the game, 11,500 fans filled Lexington's Memorial Coliseum to watch Kentucky battle Michigan State for a Final Four berth—just as more than 18,000 fans crammed into Freedom Hall to witness the Sweet Sixteen final between Lexington Lafayette and Louisville Eastern.

* * * * *

"My opinion of the Kentucky program is that it is top drawer, Park Avenue, and that all other programs in the country (only) think they are. The closest ones to it are North Carolina (and) maybe Indiana and UCLA. At Kentucky, basketball is a type of religion, such a fanatical obsession that they expect to be national champions each year and live and die with each game."
—Al McGuire, coach of Marquette's 1977 NCAA champs and a longtime television analyst

The Fabulous Five, Rupp's Runts, the Fiddlin' Five, the Unforgettables. Dan Issel, Alex Groza, Ralph Beard, Jamal Mashburn, Kyle Macy, Jack Givens, Cliff Hagan, Bill Spivey, Wah Wah Jones, Cotton Nash. Generation to generation. Native sons. Adopted ones. Black. White. They all have a place in the hearts of all Kentuckians.

Stop any number of persons on any street in Kentucky, and they'll regale and fascinate you with stories. They'll tell the stories with the swelling pride of a parent recalling a son's greatest accomplishments.

After all, they have helped rear, directly or indirectly, those young men wearing the jerseys with "KENTUCKY" printed across the front. They have participated in virtually every part of the process. They grew up playing some role in the great dream. They played little-league and junior high ball with some of the players. They saw them mature from gangly schoolboy sophomores to manly seniors. They have cheered them up close in sweaty gyms as they rose through the high school ranks. They had a good, happy cry when the players signed to play for Kentucky. And then drove hundreds of miles or journeyed halfway around the globe to cheer them on. It's their duty—and, really, their honor—to support the UK cause.

You see, they were all born to be Wildcats.

Superfan/actress Ashley Judd, placing Kentucky basketball in perspective and explaining why she skipped the Oscars for a UK game: "Life is more important than show business. The Oscars are show business. Kentucky basketball is life."

Cats Champs

1948
ncaa champions

Nine NCAA Tournaments had been played when the 1947-48 college basketball season got under way, and coach Adolph Rupp and the Kentucky Wildcats were still looking for their first national championship.

Clearly, though, the Wildcats had been a force since Rupp's arrival on the Lexington campus in the autumn of 1930. In 17 seasons under the Baron of the Bluegrass, Kentucky had fashioned a 318-68 record, won the 1946 National Invitation Tournament and made two appearances in the NCAA Tournament, whose select field was limited to eight teams in those days. And when Rupp rolled out the ball for the start of practice in the fall of '47, he was greeted by a nucleus of players that had contributed mightily to a 34-3 record the season before—standouts like center Alex Groza, guard Ralph Beard and forward Wallace "Wah Wah" Jones. Also back were talented guard Kenny Rollins and steely forward Cliff Barker, who had been a prisoner of war in World War II. UK, it seemed, had the makings of a truly fabulous five.

With Groza and Beard supplying the firepower, Kentucky overwhelmed the first seven opponents on its '47-'48 schedule—the Wildcats demoralized Tulsa, 72-18 and 71-22, on successive nights—before losing a one-point decision to Temple. UK won its next 11 games, lost to Notre Dame, and then closed the regular season on a 9-0 run. The Cats did not lose again until they played something other than collegiate competition.

Rupp's charges breezed through the Southeastern Conference Tournament, improving their record to 31-2, and drew Columbia in the NCAA tourney in New York. Jones came up big against the Lions, pouring in 21 points, and Groza and Beard combined for 32 more as the Wildcats won, 76-53, and swept into the Eastern final against defending national champion Holy Cross. Rollins put the clamps on Holy Cross' top regular-season scorer, ballhandling wizard Bob Cousy (who was limited to five points), and the 6-7 Groza broke loose for 23 points in UK's 60-52 triumph at Madison Square Garden. In the Western final, played in Kansas City, Baylor upended Kansas State by the same score.

One victory away from its first NCAA championship, Kentucky was a solid favorite against a Baylor team that had lost seven games and didn't match up well against Groza and the 6-4, 225-pound Jones. In fact, no Bears player was taller than 6-3. Sure enough, UK dominated. Baylor, working the ball

The Cats had that championship feeling in 1948—not once, but twice.

carefully in an effort to get off a good shot on every possession against its physical opponent, fell behind, 13-1, and didn't make a field goal until more than 7½ minutes had elapsed in the game. The Wildcats stormed to a 29-16 halftime lead and rolled to a 58-42 triumph at the Garden, college basketball's showplace. Groza led UK with 14 points, Beard added 12 and Jones and Rollins each had nine.

It was a magic moment for Rupp, the University of Kentucky and Big Blue fans throughout the Commonwealth. After all, NCAA championship banner No. 1 was ready to be raised. But there was even more to come in March 1948.

This was an Olympic year, and the Trials were made up of AAU and college teams. UK met up with Baylor again, routing the Bears by 18 points in the semifinals, but the Cats lost to the Phillips Oilers and 7-foot Bob Kurland in the title game. Still, Kentucky's starting five—forever known in UK lore as the Fabulous Five—was named to the 14-man U.S. Olympic squad, a team that brought home the gold medal.

The Cats had that championship feeling in 1948—not once, but twice.

When Adolph Rupp received the winner's trophy on behalf of Kentucky's first national championship team, it was a heady experience for the Cats and their fans, who soon grew accustomed to such ceremonies.

1949

ncaa champions

After reaching the summit of the college basketball world the previous season, the Kentucky Wildcats weren't about to take a back seat to anyone in 1948-49. The Cats, who with the exception of guard Kenny Rollins had every key player back from their first NCAA championship squad, were cruising along with an 8-0 record entering the title game of the holiday Sugar Bowl Tournament in New Orleans. They had won six of their games by 27 or more points.

The aura of invincibility ended on December 30, 1948, though, when the Ed Macauley-led Saint Louis Billikens, unbeaten and coming off an NIT crown, rallied from a 27-18 halftime deficit and edged the Wildcats, 42-40, in a game that produced a flurry of UK misplays in the late going. Kentucky suffered another indignity three weeks later when the first wire-service college basketball poll in history was released, with the Associated Press rankings listing UK No. 2, behind Saint Louis. But the poll's top two spots would flip-flop within two weeks, with Kentucky reasserting itself with a burst of standout play that carried through the SEC Tournament in early March. A 68-52 victory over Tulane in the SEC championship game—in which Wildcats center Alex Groza went on a 37-point spree—was UK's 21st consecutive win.

Next up for Adolph Rupp's team was a berth in the NIT, an appearance that did not preclude Kentucky's participation in the NCAA Tournament. Despite its glittering 29-1 record and No. 1 ranking, UK came out uncharacteristically flat against Loyola of Chicago in a first-round game. The Ramblers, ranked 16th in the final AP poll of the season, upset the Wildcats, 67-56, with UK frontcourt stars Groza and Wah Wah Jones combining for only 18 points. Meanwhile, Loyola's Jack Kerris, who finished with 23 points, seemed to score at will. Bounced from the NIT, the Wildcats went home to Lexington to prepare for the NCAA Tournament—and prepare they did under stern taskmaster Rupp, who was none too pleased with the Cats' listless effort against Loyola.

With redemption in mind, the Wildcats returned to the scene of their pratfall, Madison Square Garden, home of the NIT and once again host for the NCAA Tournament's Eastern playoffs. The Cats were matched against high-scoring Paul Arizin and Villanova, which boasted a 22-3 record. Arizin was as good as advertised. Saddled with four first-half fouls as his team fell behind, 48-37, at intermission, he scored 19 second-half points and finished with 30 overall before fouling out in the final 2 minutes. Only

UK was college basketball's top cat, two years running.

problem was, Groza was his equal—and Alex had considerably more support. Groza scored 30 points, UK forward Jim Line contributed 21 and Cats swingman Cliff Barker added 18. Kentucky won, 85-72, and advanced to the NCAA Eastern final against Illinois.

Kentucky was on top of its game against Illinois, which was rated the nation's No. 4 team in the AP's last balloting. Playing with deft precision on offense and stifling pressure on defense, the Wildcats smothered the Illini, 76-47. Groza again was impossible to contain, scoring 27 points. Now, only one team, Oklahoma A&M, separated the Kentucky Wildcats from back-to-back national crowns, and to that point A&M was the only team to score an NCAA "double." Henry Iba's Aggies had won national championships in 1945 and 1946.

Iba preached stingy defense—and his players were true believers. In reaching the NCAA final, to be contested at the University of Washington in Seattle, Oklahoma A&M had defeated Wyoming, 40-39, and Oregon State, 55-30.

As it turned out, it was Rupp's team that played suffocating defense when the chips were down. The Cats, up 25-20 at halftime, held A&M to 16 second-half points and pulled away to a 46-36 triumph. Groza repeatedly outmaneuvered the man Iba hoped would neutralize him, 6-7 Bob Harris, for 25 points. No other UK player had more than five. Harris, nearly 30 pounds lighter than Groza, finished with only seven points.

UK was college basketball's top cat, two years running.

In a 1949 NCAA Tournament win over Villanova, Alex Groza (No. 15, right) scored 30 points and was a force on the boards. Jim Line (25) added 21 points. Paul Arizin (11) had 30 for the losers.

1951
ncaa champions

Kentuckians were plenty miffed when their beloved Wildcats were denied a shot at a third consecutive NCAA championship in 1949-50. The Cats, featuring 7-foot sensation Bill Spivey, had won 25 of 30 games and finished third in the final AP national rankings. Yet an NCAA selection committee chose North Carolina State, rated No. 5 in the nation, to represent the district in whose boundaries Kentucky lay. The Cats were left with the option of playing in the NIT, and they accepted the invitation. It was an R.S.V.P. hardly worth making—UK was embarrassed, 89-50, by a CCNY team that went on to win both the NIT crown and NCAA title in March 1950.

No other school could claim three NCAA championship plaques in its trophy case.

Adolph Rupp and company pointed toward 1950-51, a season in which the Wildcats moved from cozy Alumni Gym (capacity: 2,800) to their new basketball palace, 11,500-seat Memorial Coliseum. New teammates for Spivey included sophomore standouts Frank Ramsey, a guard/forward, and versatile frontcourt player Cliff Hagan. Forwards Shelby Linville and Walt Hirsch and guard Bobby Watson were key holdovers. With the NCAA Tournament field expanding from eight to 16 teams, there appeared to be no way to exclude UK from the tourney this time around. And the Wildcats made certain of their inclusion.

After being upended by Saint Louis for the second time in three seasons in the late-December Sugar Bowl Tournament, Kentucky's basketball machine churned out 21 consecutive victories before falling to Vanderbilt, 61-57, in the title game of the SEC Tournament. A week earlier, UK had concluded the SEC regular season at 14-0 with a 32-point spanking of the Commodores.

With an NCAA Tournament bid safely in hand but minus the services of Hirsch, ruled ineligible for postseason play because he was a fourth-year varsity player, Kentucky opened the tournament against state neighbor Louisville, which it had played only once since 1922—and that meeting had come in the 1948 Olympic Trials. UK didn't shoot well—Spivey, Ramsey, Hagan, Linville and Lou Tsioropoulos were a combined 18 for 65 (28 percent) from the field—but the Cats prevailed, 79-68, in Raleigh, N.C. Linville finished with 23 points and 10 rebounds, Ramsey had 14 points and 15 rebounds and guard Lucian Whitaker, who was locked in, made eight of 15 floor shots for 16 points.

The victory vaulted Kentucky into the Eastern semifinals in New York, where the Wildcats dispatched St. John's, 59-43, and Illinois knocked off North Carolina State. The results set up a rematch of the 1949 Eastern final, in which UK thrashed the Fighting Illini by 29 points. This time, it was razor-close. The Cats, overcoming a seven-point halftime deficit, slipped past Illinois, 76-74, when Linville hit a late shot and Illinois' Don Sunderlage followed with a miss as the clock wound down. Spivey came on strong in the second half and finished with 28 points and 16 rebounds.

In the Western final at Kansas City, highly touted Kansas State routed Oklahoma A&M, 68-44, and improved its record to a gaudy 25-3. Kentucky's mark was even gaudier at 31-2.

The Wildcats from the Plains were given a reasonable chance of defeating the Wildcats from the Commonwealth in the national final—despite Kentucky's No. 1 ranking and impressive depth (four UK players, led by Spivey's 19.2 figure, boasted double-figure scoring averages and two others were notching nine points per game). Hagan's game-day throat infection added more intrigue to the title clash, played in Minneapolis, but Hagan came out of sick bay and helped rally Kentucky after Kansas State jumped to an early lead. K-State still nursed a two-point edge at halftime, but Spivey asserted himself in the second half and helped UK seize control. He finished with 22 points and 21 rebounds as Kentucky posted a 68-58 win.

Tradition-rich University of Kentucky basketball was getting richer. No other school could claim three NCAA championship plaques in its trophy case, and UK had put them there in a four-year span.

The Wildcats were ecstatic after winning their way into the 1951 NCAA title game with a 76-74 victory over Illinois in the Eastern final.

1958
ncaa champions

As Kentucky's 1957-58 season neared, the university's national championship days seemed distant. No, March 1951 wasn't all that long ago. But the intervening years seemed to pass interminably, with one dose of bad news following another.

Most disturbing of all was word in October 1951 that a widespread college basketball gambling scandal had reached the University of Kentucky program. Among those implicated in the point-shaving and fixing schemes were former Wildcats stars Alex Groza and Ralph Beard. The scandal also touched ex-Cats Dale Barnstable, Walt Hirsch and Jim Line, and it took down Bill Spivey before he had completed his eligibility at UK (although Spivey, in fact, was never proved guilty of any offense). Many games—including the surprising NIT loss to Loyola of Chicago in 1949 and close defeats at the hands of Saint Louis in the late '40s and early 1950s—were pinpointed by authorities for wrongdoing, or highly questionable behavior, on the part of Kentucky players. Once the mess was sorted out, the NCAA placed UK basketball in mothballs for the 1952-53 season because of major infractions dating to 1948.

Once the good times returned, disappointment wasn't far behind. After its one-season banishment, Kentucky returned to the court in 1953-54 and once again rose to the heights. The Wildcats had a perfect record, 25-0—but an imperfect end to their season. With leading players Cliff Hagan, Frank Ramsey and Lou Tsioropoulos barred from the NCAA Tournament because they were graduate students—those three had spent their senior years playing intrasquad games—UK declined to enter the tourney.

Talented-but-not-great Cats teams then won 66 of 80 games over the next three seasons, but they failed to advance beyond NCAA regional play. The '57-'58 squad had potential, to be sure, but it wound up only No. 9 in the season's final AP poll. Yet this plucky bunch, beaten six times overall during the regular season, kept alive its hope of restoring glory to UK basketball by winning the Southeastern Conference title and qualifying for the NCAA Tournament. And with the Mideast Regional scheduled on the Wildcats' home court and the Final Four to be played in Louisville, anything appeared possible.

Coach Adolph Rupp, his team playing what he called a "Carnegie Hall" schedule, probably wasn't so optimistic. "We've got fiddlers, that's all," he had said earlier. "They're pretty good fiddlers. (They'd) be all right entertaining at a barn dance. But I tell you, you need a violinist to play in Carnegie Hall. We don't have any violinists."

But the "Fiddlin' Five," as the team became

"We've got fiddlers, that's all. ... But I tell you, you need a violinist to play in Carnegie Hall."

known, did have heady players in senior guard Vernon Hatton and junior forward Johnny Cox and a balanced attack featuring four starters who scored in double figures. And this was a resilient bunch, one that never doubted itself after losing three of its first seven games.

The Lexington regional proved to be a romp for UK. Ten Cats, led by Cox's 23 points and Adrian Smith's 18, reached the scoring column in a 94-70 pasting of Miami of Ohio, and 10 also made the scoring sheet in an 89-56 rout of Notre Dame. Hatton stung the Fighting Irish with 26 points.

In the Final Four semifinals, Kentucky went against Temple, a team it had beaten in three overtimes in the first week of the season. A highlight of the earlier meeting was Hatton's 47-foot tying shot at the end of the first overtime.

In the rematch at Freedom Hall, Temple led, 60-57, in the final minute, but two free throws by Smith and Hatton's driving layup lifted UK to a stunning 61-60 triumph. Seattle, powered by Elgin Baylor, walloped Kansas State in the other semifinal.

Rupp questioned whether the Cats could contain Baylor, the man of confounding fakes and moves, but the Chieftains' superstar got into foul trouble against UK in the title game and was further hampered by sore ribs. Kentucky, down by 11 points early and trailing by three at halftime, charged back, with Cox's 16 points in the final 15 minutes leading the blitz. Cox wound up with 24 points, Hatton got 30 and John Crigler scored 14. Kentucky won, 84-72, for its fourth NCAA crown and last under Rupp.

"This team (which failed to land a player on the All-SEC first team) played the best, as a unit, of any of the championship teams I've coached," said Rupp, who no doubt could hear violinists in the distance.

Fighting for the ball in the 1958 NCAA title game, Kentucky's John Crigler soared into the air between Seattle players Charley Brown (No. 45) and Jerry Frizzell. UK's Johnny Cox (alongside Frizzell, arms extended) was hoping to latch on. Cox sparked the Wildcats with 16 points in the game's final 15 minutes.

1978
ncaa champions

When Joe B. Hall succeeded the legendary Adolph Rupp as coach of the Kentucky Wildcats after the 1971-72 season, he knew he was entering a big-time pressure situation. Then, after five seasons of failing to guide Kentucky to a national championship, Hall knew he had to win the top prize—and soon—to satisfy the basketball-crazed populace of the Commonwealth.

Never mind that the great Rupp himself did not win an NCAA title in his final 14 seasons in Lexington. The pertinent facts, as the 1977-78 season dawned, were these: Kentucky had captured four national crowns, all under Rupp, but UK had not won it all in nearly two decades. The drought was unacceptable.

It wasn't that Hall was underachieving. He coached the Wildcats to the 1975 NCAA title game, twice came within one victory of the Final Four and led the Cats to the 1976 NIT championship.

The outlook was promising for '77-'78. Twin towers Rick Robey and Mike Phillips and midsized forwards Jack Givens and James Lee were back for their senior years, solid guard Truman Claytor also was returning and Purdue transfer Kyle Macy was about to make his debut in the Kentucky backcourt. And the Cats were coming off a 26-4 season.

Ranked second behind North Carolina in the AP's preseason poll, Kentucky moved to No. 1 after the first week of play and held the top spot for 11 consecutive weeks. The Wildcats won their first 14 games—Indiana, Kansas, St. John's and Notre Dame were among the victims—and topped the 100-point mark five times. Alabama put an end to the winning streak on January 23 in Tuscaloosa, and LSU upset UK in overtime 2½ weeks later in Baton Rouge. Hall's team then closed out the regular season with eight consecutive victories, improving its record to 25-2.

The Cats opened the NCAA Tournament in Knoxville, Tenn., against a Florida State team that wasn't impressed with UK's press clippings. The Seminoles bolted to a 39-32 halftime lead, but Kentucky's depth and firepower proved too much in the final 20 minutes. Reserves Dwane Casey, Fred Cowan and LaVon Williams played key minutes for UK at the start of the second half, their fresh legs pumping vitality into the Cats' defense. The Seminoles withered. The Wildcats wound up winning, 85-76, with six UK players scoring in double figures. Claytor led the way with 16 points and Phillips and Macy added 14 each.

The Wildcats won their first 14 games—Indiana, Kansas, St. John's and Notre Dame were among the victims—and topped the 100-point mark five times.

The Kentucky-Florida State winner was expected to play defending national champion Marquette in a Mideast Regional semifinal in Dayton, Ohio, but UK caught a break when Marquette was upset by Miami of Ohio. The Mid-American Conference champion was no match for the Wildcats, falling 91-69.

UK's opponent in the Mideast final would be considerably more formidable. The foe was Michigan State, which had won the Big Ten title behind the exploits of Greg Kelser, Jay Vincent and freshman wunderkind Earvin "Magic" Johnson. The Spartans slowed Kentucky's high-octane offense with an aggressive zone defense and took a 27-22 halftime lead. But UK made two key adjustments: Shot-producing screens would be set for Macy, and the Wildcats would switch from a man-to-man defense to a zone. Both moves had a telling effect. Macy got open for shots and drew key fouls—he sank four free throws in the final 39 seconds—and Michigan State managed only 22 second-half points. The Spartans' Johnson made only two of 10 floor shots and turned the ball over six times. Kentucky won, 52-49, and advanced to the Final Four in St. Louis.

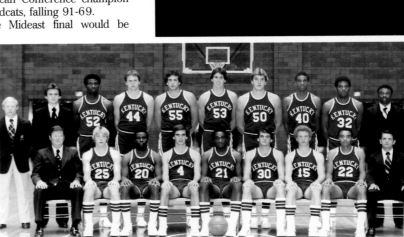

The Wildcats got another big test in the national semifinals, slipping past Arkansas, 64-59. Then, matched against a young Duke team in the championship game, the experience-savvy Cats made another critical decision. With Duke employing a 2-3 zone and stretching it from the baseline, Hall reasoned that the Blue Devils would be vulnerable in the middle. They were. UK repeatedly went to Givens, who maneuvered his way to the foul-line area, and the quick 6-4 player put up 27 shots and scored 41 points. Despite a spirited Duke bid, Kentucky ended its national-title drought with a 94-88 victory.

Hall, at last, found time to relax.

Towering Rick Robey took a back seat to Jack Givens in the 1978 NCAA final, but he came up big with 20 points and 11 rebounds.

1996
ncaa champions

In June 1989, Rick Pitino took over a Kentucky basketball program that had been placed on NCAA probation for three years. The penalties meted out by the NCAA (which included a two-year ban from postseason play)—and the accompanying UK player defections—left Wildcats basketball in tatters.

But Pitino quickly restored honor and prestige to UK basketball. His first team managed a 14-14 record, a mark that proved almost uplifting after Eddie Sutton's Cats finished 13-19 the year before. Kentucky then posted records of 22-6, 29-7, 30-4, 27-7 and 28-5. Pitino's 1992-93 squad reached the Final Four, and two other Pitino-coached UK teams came within one victory of reaching college basketball's showcase event.

Pitino quickly restored honor and prestige to UK basketball.

The Cats had numerous returnees on hand entering the 1995-96 season, with Tony Delk, Walter McCarty, Antoine Walker, Mark Pope, Anthony Epps and Jeff Sheppard heading the list. Newcomers included highly touted Ohio State transfer Derek Anderson and heralded freshmen Ron Mercer and Wayne Turner.

Kentucky, ranked No. 1 in the Associated Press' preseason poll, got the season off to a rousing start with a 96-84 triumph over Maryland in the Tip-Off Classic in Springfield, Mass. Pope, a 6-10 center, and Delk, a guard and UK's leading scorer the previous two seasons, scored 26 and 21 points, respectively. But Massachusetts, which later in the season would spend two months as the nation's top-ranked team, brought the Cats back to earth four days later. UMass bolted to a 29-10 lead en route to a 92-82 victory. Even in that defeat, though, the Cats showed their mettle. Kentucky hit six 3-pointers in rallying to tie the score by halftime, and it trailed by only two points with 3:45 remaining in the game before running out of counters to Marcus Camby.

From that point on, the Wildcats went about their business with extraordinary skill, precision and passion. They defeated Indiana, 89-82, before 41,071 fans at the RCA Dome in Indianapolis and then beat Wisconsin-Green Bay, 74-62, before winning their next 12 games by 17 or more points. A relatively close call occurred on January 24 at Athens, Ga., when Tubby Smith's Georgia Bulldogs battled back from a 14-point second-half deficit and tied the game with less than nine minutes remaining. But sophomore swingman Allen Edwards and guards Delk and Epps scored key points in the late going that enabled UK to pull out an 82-77 win.

Having gotten a scare, Kentucky returned to its devastating ways and won its next 12 games -- all against Southeastern Conference rivals -- by margins of 32, 14, 39, 15, 13, 40, 19, 31, 15, 38, 24 and 20 points. The Cats, who had run the table in the SEC and won the Eastern Division by seven games (runner-up Georgia was 9-7, compared to UK's 16-0), entered the SEC Tournament championship game against Mississippi State with a 27-game winning streak. The Bulldogs, SEC Western champs, broke open a tight game with a 14-2 run at the outset of the second half and dealt UK an 84-73 defeat.

Like the early-season loss to UMass, the pre-NCAA Tournament setback against Mississippi State was a mere blip on Kentucky's sky's-the-limit radar screen. UK rolled into the Final Four for the 11th time in school history by blitzing tourney opponents San Jose State (110-72), Virginia Tech (84-60), Utah (101-70) and Wake Forest (83-63). All of which set up a rematch against Massachusetts in the national semifinals in East Rutherford, N.J.

This time, it was UMass that fell behind early, and the Minutemen dug themselves into a 15-point hole two minutes into the second half before closing the gap to three points in the late going. That's as close as UMass could get. Kentucky, getting 20 points from Delk, 14 from Walker and eight points and 10 rebounds from McCarty, held on for an 81-74 victory. Camby, who had scorched the Cats for 32 points in November, scored 25 this time.

UK also got Syracuse into deep trouble in the national title game, taking a 13-point lead with just over 11 minutes to play. Like UMass, the Orangemen roared back. A 16-5 run pulled Syracuse within two points at 64-62, but McCarty's tip-in of an errant Delk shot and Anderson's 3-point field goal gave the Wildcats a safe lead. Kentucky, fueled by Delk's seven 3-pointers and 20 off-the-bench points from Mercer, won, 76-67, for its sixth national crown.

Pitino, who now had brought UK basketball all the way back, proclaimed these Cats "The Untouchables"—a fitting label for a team that went 34-2 and won its NCAA tourney games by an average margin of 21.5 points.

Rick Pitino's "Untouchables" featured numerous returnees and some talented newcomers. UK capped a 34-2 season with a 76-67 win over Syracuse in the NCAA title game.

1998
ncaa champions

It had been nearly 50 years since the Kentucky Wildcats were this formidable. The Cats had won the NCAA championship in 1996 and reached the title game in 1997, only to lose in overtime. Plus, they had come within one game of making the Final Four in 1995. UK's cumulative record under Rick Pitino over those three seasons: 97-12.

Pitino wasn't around when the 1997-98 season got under way, though. Also among the missing were Ron Mercer and Derek Anderson, Kentucky's top two scorers in 1996-97. All were off to the pros—Pitino as coach of the Boston Celtics and Mercer and Anderson as the sixth and 13th picks overall in the NBA draft. Mercer had left UK after his sophomore season; Anderson had used up his collegiate eligibility.

No matter.

Pitino was succeeded by highly regarded Georgia coach Tubby Smith, who had served on the UK staff before becoming head coach at Tulsa and then Georgia. Guard Jeff Sheppard, who was redshirted in the 1996-97, and center Nazr Mohammed stepped to the fore in '97-'98 and received excellent support from forwards Scott Padgett and Allen Edwards and point guard Wayne Turner. Frontcourt players Jamaal Magloire and Heshimu Evans (a transfer from Manhattan) also made major contributions.

The result was another banner—as in championship banner—season for the Wildcats. And it was achieved in no small way because of an excellent coaching job by Smith, who somehow made the whole of this team much greater than the sum of its parts. (The Cats had only one player, Mohammed, on the Associated Press' All-Southeastern Conference first team, and they placed none on AP's second team.)

If this team lacked superstars—and it did—the Wildcats more than made up for it with a team concept that emphasized role players. An early-season loss to Arizona, UK's conqueror in the NCAA title game the previous March, and three regular-season defeats at Rupp Arena never fazed this group. In fact, Smith's Cats carried a 26-4 record into the SEC Tournament in Atlanta and served notice that they would be a force in the NCAA tourney. Kentucky defeated Alabama in the SEC opener, then coasted to victory against Arkansas in the semifinals after jumping to a 58-33 halftime lead. In the championship game, the Cats buried South Carolina by 30 points.

It was on to the NCAA Tournament, whose South Regional first- and second-round games were scheduled at the Georgia Dome—the same venue that played host to the SEC tourney. Kentucky, on familiar ground, eliminated South Carolina State and Saint Louis and advanced to a South Regional semifinal meeting against UCLA in St. Petersburg,

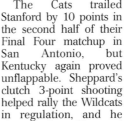

Fla. With Padgett scoring 19 points, Sheppard 16 and Mohammed 15, UK overwhelmed the Bruins, 94-68, in a game featuring six blocked shots each by Mohammed and Magloire, UK's 6-10 enforcers.

The South Regional championship game paired Kentucky and Duke, teams that had played a classic regional title game six years earlier—the one decided in overtime by a turnaround jump shot by the Blue Devils' Christian Laettner. This time, it appeared that Duke would need no such heroics. The Blue Devils held a 17-point lead with less than 10 minutes remaining in the game. But with Turner proving the catalyst and Evans, Padgett and sharpshooter Cameron Mills offering significant help, the Wildcats steadily chipped away at the deficit and came out 86-84 winners.

The result was another banner—as in championship banner—season for the Wildcats.

The Cats trailed Stanford by 10 points in the second half of their Final Four matchup in San Antonio, but Kentucky again proved unflappable. Sheppard's clutch 3-point shooting helped rally the Wildcats in regulation, and he sank a crucial 3-pointer in overtime. Sheppard finished with 27 points in the national semifinal game as Kentucky pulled out another one, 86-85. Then, down by 10 points against Utah at halftime of the NCAA championship game, UK rallied once more. Reserves Evans and Mills and the veteran Sheppard did yeoman work in the final 20 minutes—Evans scored eight consecutive points early in the second half—and Kentucky won, 78-69, for its seventh NCAA crown. The deficit was the largest halftime margin ever overcome in the title game.

It was another great moment for Kentucky basketball. For coach Smith, it was the best of times—one season as UK coach, one NCAA crown to his credit.

It may have been cut-up time when a team picture was taken (opposite page), but the 1997-98 Cats were all business on the court. UK, which got a remarkable coaching job all season from Tubby Smith, overcame sizable deficits in the South Regional final, the national semifinals and the NCAA championship game to win its seventh national title. Smith, athletic director C.M. Newton and the Wildcats savored the moment.

Other Winners

1933 HELMS ATHLETIC FOUNDATION NATIONAL CHAMPIONS

Kentucky's first true national championship team was Adolph Rupp's 1947-48 squad, which won the NCAA Tournament. But the 1932-33 Wildcats, who predated the tournament, also were recognized as the nation's No. 1 team. Those Cats were proclaimed national champions by the prestigious, Los Angeles-based Helms Athletic Foundation, which was founded later in the 1930s and retroactively bestowed national-title and All-American status on those it considered rightful teams and players.

The '32-'33 Cats won 21 of 24 games in Rupp's third season as UK coach, went unbeaten in the new Southeastern Conference and swept through the league tournament by winning four games by an average margin of 18.5 points.

Frontcourt players Forest Sale (Kentucky's first consensus All-American) and John DeMoisey were double-figure scorers at a time when such an output by two players on one team was relatively rare. Sale averaged 13.8 points and DeMoisey scored 12 points per game.

Other leading players on the team were guards Bill Davis and Ellis Johnson, forward Darrell Darby and center George Yates.

1954 HELMS ATHLETIC FOUNDATION NATIONAL CHAMPIONS

La Salle captured the NCAA Tournament title in 1954, so, naturally, everyone considered the Explorers the No. 1 team in the land, right? Not by a long shot.

Adolph Rupp's Kentucky team got the nod from two major sources—the Helms Athletic Foundation and the Associated Press, which for only the second time conducted its final poll of the season after the tournament. Those entities, clearly of the opinion that no team could quite measure up to UK, saw no reason to penalize the Wildcats for rejecting a bid to play in the NCAA Tournament, a refusal that came on the heels of an edict barring Kentucky standouts Cliff Hagan, Frank Ramsey and Lou Tsioropoulos from NCAA postseason play because of their status as graduate students.

Hagan, Ramsey and Tsioropoulos, limited to intrasquad games as UK seniors because of a one-season basketball "death penalty" imposed on the university for various NCAA violations, were unstoppable in 1953-54 as Kentucky manhandled opponents on the way to a 25-0 season. Hagan averaged 24 points and 13.5 rebounds, Ramsey posted scoring and rebounding figures of 19.6 and 8.8 and Tsioropoulos finished at 14.5 and 9.6. Billy Evans, Gayle Rose, Phil Grawemeyer and Linville Puckett were other key members of a team that won by double-digit margins 23 times.

As it turned out, one of UK's sizable triumphs was particularly meaningful—and rewarding. It was an early-season 73-60 victory over La Salle.

1946 NIT CHAMPIONS

When Kentucky high school standouts Ralph Beard and Wallace "Wah Wah" Jones arrived on the Lexington campus in the fall of 1945, optimism ran high. True, center Alex Groza, who had arrived with considerable fanfare a year earlier, was in the military. But with Beard, Jones and another newcomer, Joe Holland, joining holdovers Jack Parkinson, Jack Tingle and Wilber Schu, UK appeared capable of riding roughshod over the opposition. And Kentucky did just that.

After losing only to Temple and Notre Dame in its first 15 games, Adolph Rupp's team never lost again. The Wildcats capped their season-ending, 15-game winning streak by capturing the National Invitation Tournament title at New York's Madison Square Garden. Jones, Parkinson and Tingle combined for 43 points as Kentucky walloped Arizona, 77-53, in the quarterfinals, and Tingle's 16 points and Beard's 15 helped UK get past West Virginia, 59-51, in the semifinals.

The NIT championship game, against Rhode Island, was not the walk in the park that the experts expected it to be. UK streaked ahead, 23-16, but the pesky Rams rebounded to take a 27-26 halftime lead. In a game featuring 11 lead changes, Rhode Island nursed a one-point edge with 2 minutes to play, but free throws by Kenton Campbell and Beard enabled Kentucky to escape with a 46-45 victory. Beard and Jones, the gifted freshmen from whom so much had been expected four months earlier, led UK in scoring with 13 and 10 points, respectively, as the Wildcats completed their season with a sparkling 28-2 record.

1976 NIT CHAMPIONS

One year after playing—and losing—in the NCAA Tournament championship game, coach Joe B. Hall's Kentucky Wildcats were back in a title game in March 1976. This time, it was the NIT.

It wasn't exactly what the Cats, always aiming high, had in mind at the outset of the season. Yet, in view of the departure of Kevin Grevey, Jimmy Dan Conner, Mike Flynn and Bob Guyette from the team that had lost to UCLA in the 1975 NCAA final, it was a notable accomplishment.

For a good portion of the season, the 1975-76 Wildcats appeared to be headed nowhere for the postseason—except back to Lexington—as one lackluster effort followed another. Kentucky opened with two defeats, had a 5-6 record on January 10 and stood at 10-10 in mid-February. After a loss at Vanderbilt on February 14, UK saw its Southeastern Conference record dip to 5-7.

But with sophomores Jack Givens, Mike Phillips, James Lee and Rick Robey maturing, and junior Larry Johnson and senior Reggie Warford making sizable contributions, Kentucky won its last six SEC games and received an invitation to the NIT. Its confidence high, UK reached the title game with victories over Niagara, Kansas State and Providence. In the final against UNC Charlotte, the Wildcats got a big lift from Warford, the lone senior on the squad, and won, 71-67. Warford, who hadn't scored in the previous two games, broke loose for 14 in this one, sinking seven of 10 field-goal attempts. Phillips and Johnson each had 16 points.

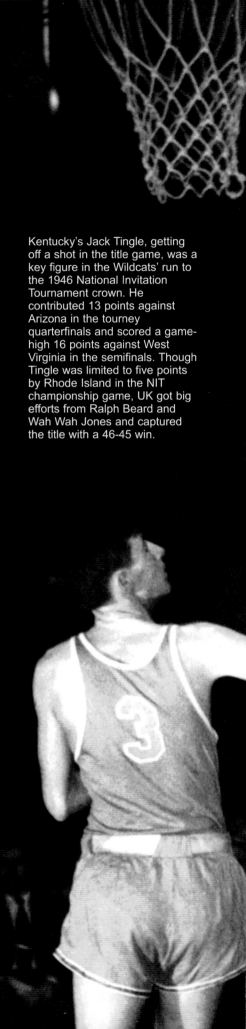

Kentucky's Jack Tingle, getting off a shot in the title game, was a key figure in the Wildcats' run to the 1946 National Invitation Tournament crown. He contributed 13 points against Arizona in the tourney quarterfinals and scored a game-high 16 points against West Virginia in the semifinals. Though Tingle was limited to five points by Rhode Island in the NIT championship game, UK got big efforts from Ralph Beard and Wah Wah Jones and captured the title with a 46-45 win.

Legendary Teams

THE FABULOUS FIVE

They were aptly named. Center Alex Groza, forwards Cliff Barker and Wah Wah Jones and guards Ralph Beard and Kenny Rollins were positively fabulous during the 1947-48 season, earning their collective nickname in the course of a season in which they led Kentucky to 36 victories in 39 games and the NCAA Tournament championship. Not only that, the entire UK starting five was a key part of the 1948 U.S. Olympic team that won the gold medal in London—and Groza was the U.S. squad's leading scorer in the Games.

Groza and Beard averaged a team-high 12.5 points for Kentucky, which went 9-0 in Southeastern Conference play and capped a 16-game winning streak with a victory over Baylor in the NCAA title game.

THE FIDDLIN' FIVE

Coach Adolph Rupp said his 1957-58 Kentucky players were "pretty good fiddlers," but he insisted his team needed a violinist or two if the Wildcats were to succeed in the face of a daunting schedule.

These Cats, a tenacious group with a strong work ethic, used a quintessential team concept to make up for any shortcomings they might have had. And when all was said and done, UK's fiddlers played beautiful music—they won the school's fourth NCAA championship.

Guards Vernon Hatton and Adrian Smith, center Ed Beck and forwards Johnny Cox and John Crigler made it happen in UK's 23-6 season. Hatton was the big gun offensively, averaging 17.1 points, and Cox scored 14.9 points per game. And Cox, Beck and Crigler were relentless on the boards, averaging 12.6, 11.6 and 9.9 rebounds, respectively.

RUPP'S RUNTS

Kentucky's starting unit in 1965-66 was made up of 6-foot Louie Dampier and 6-5 Tommy Kron at guard, 6-4 Pat Riley and 6-3 Larry Conley at forward and 6-5 Thad Jaracz at center. There was no question about the derivation of this team's nickname. And there was no question about the depth of this team's competitiveness, either.

Small only in physical stature, this team had a remarkable season. The Wildcats fashioned a 15-1 record in the Southeastern Conference and finished 27-2 overall. With all five starters boasting double-figure scoring averages (led by Riley's 22 points per game and Dampier's 21.1 mark), Kentucky was atop the wire-service polls at the end of the regular season. Yet these Cats fell short where it counted most—in the NCAA title game. But even after UK's 72-65 loss to Texas Western, this undersized and gutty team remained darlings of the Common-wealth.

THE UNFORGETTABLES

They weren't national champions. They weren't gifted athletes. But they were truly unforgettable.

Having encountered the three-year probation dealt to the Kentucky basketball program by the NCAA—UK was barred from postseason play for two years—John Pelphrey, Richie Farmer, Deron Feldhaus and Sean Woods weathered the tough times when they could have avoided them by leaving the university. Loyalty kept these four players at UK, and perseverance carried them through—much to the admiration of Kentucky fans everywhere.

In their senior season, 1991-92, the four players teamed with sophomore sensation Jamal Mashburn to take the Cats to heights that few thought possible. Kentucky went 29-7 that season, missing a berth in the Final Four when Christian Laettner's shot at the buzzer gave Duke a 104-103 overtime victory over the Wildcats in the NCAA East Regional final.

Dogged seniors John Pelphrey (far right), Richie Farmer, Deron Feldhaus and Sean Woods needed a star to make the 1991-92 Cats a formidable team—and Jamal Mashburn (right) was their man.

Other Great Teams

Championship teams rate special niches in Kentucky lore, but there have been many other great teams in the 100 years of UK basketball. Among the most memorable:

TEAM ACCOMPLISHMENT

1911-12: Compiled a 9-0 record in the 10th season of Kentucky Wildcats basketball.

1913-14: Victorious in its last eight games and fashioned a 12-2 record.

1920-21: Won 13 of 14 games. Only defeat: a two-point loss to Centre.

1931-32: Ran off a 14-game winning streak on the way to a 15-2 record.

1933-34: Unbeaten until upset by Florida in the SEC Tournament. Finished 16-1.

1934-35: Won its first four games by 47, 69, 29 and 40 points en route to a 19-2 mark.

1941-42: Made its first appearance in the NCAA Tournament, lost to Dartmouth in the national semifinals. Wound up 19-6.

1943-44: Finished third in the NIT. Had a 13-game winning streak in a 19-2 season.

1944-45: Won its first 11 games, later had a 7-0 run. Record: 22-4.

1946-47: Outscored opponents by an average of 30 points while winning 34 of 37 games. Was 11-0 in the SEC. Fell to Utah in the NIT championship game.

1951-52: Finished atop the Associated Press and United Press final polls, conducted before the NCAA Tournament. Was 14-0 in the SEC. Lost to St. John's in the NCAA East Regional final (one victory away from the Final Four) and finished 29-3.

1954-55: Went 23-3 and was ranked No. 2 in the final wire-service polls.

1958-59: Won its first 11 games, went 13-3 the rest of the way.

1961-62: Won 16 in a row in one stretch and was 13-1 in the SEC. Finished 23-3. Was one victory away from the Final Four.

1965-66: Ranked No. 1 in both final wire-service polls, conducted before the completion of the NCAA Tournament. Was 23-0 before losing at Tennessee. Finished 15-1 in the SEC. Beaten by Texas Western in the NCAA final and finished 27-2.

1969-70: Ranked No. 1 in both final wire-service polls, conducted before the completion of the NCAA Tournament. Started out 15-0, finished at 26-2. Posted a 17-1 SEC mark. One win away from the Final Four, was ousted from the NCAA tourney by Jacksonville, 106-100. Reached the 100-point mark 13 times.

1974-75: Lost to UCLA, 92-85, in the NCAA Tournament title game. Record: 26-5.

1976-77: Won 26 of 30 games. Eliminated from the NCAA tourney by North Carolina in the East Regional final.

1979-80: 29-6 team had winning streaks of 12 and 11 games.

1983-84: Compiled a 29-5 mark. Defeated by Georgetown in a Final Four semifinal game.

1985-86: Won 32 games, lost four. Put together a 17-1 record in the SEC. Beaten by LSU in the NCAA Southeast Regional final.

1991-92: Lost to Duke in the NCAA East Regional final on Christian Laettner's turnaround jump shot in overtime. Defeat was its seventh against 29 wins.

1992-93: Reached the Final Four but fell to Michigan in the semifinals. Record: 30-4.

1994-95: Finished 14-2 in the SEC and 28-5 overall but fell one victory short of the Final Four.

1996-97: Lost in overtime to Arizona in the NCAA title game. Won 35 of 40 games.

1998-99: Postseason run fell one victory short of the Final Four for a 28-9 team.

The 1992-93 Cats featuring Tony Delk, Jamal Mashburn, Travis Ford and Jared Prickett (No. 32) lost to Jalen Rose (5) and Michigan in the Final Four.

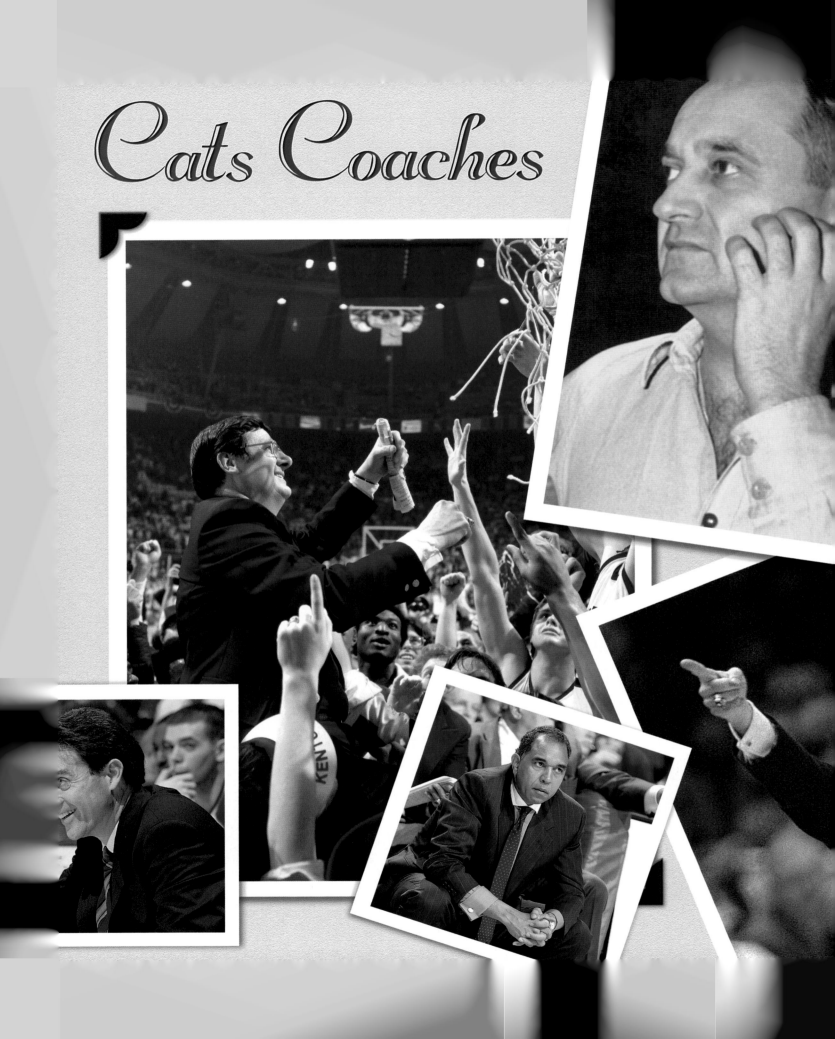

Cats Coaches

adolph rupp

Rupp.

No other word carries so much weight and meaning to Kentucky basketball—or serves as such a lightning rod for college basketball historians and analysts. One of the greatest coaches in the sport's history, Adolph Rupp was a complicated man who remains a fascinating personality 25 years after his death.

Though Rupp was Kansas-born and educated in the classroom and on the court in the Sunflower State, he is synonymous with Kentucky. In 41 seasons at the helm of the UK basketball team, "the man in the brown suit" created a program that won at an amazing rate and thereby imbued the entire state with an enormous sense of pride.

Rupp's teams captured four NCAA championships and one NIT title (when the New York tourney was a prestigious affair). His Wildcats won 876 games and chalked up a winning percentage of .822. They were Southeastern Conference champions 27 times.

The Baron of the Bluegrass was born in 1901 in Halstead, Kan., and he played under the legendary Phog Allen at the University of Kansas. Rupp later defeated his mentor in their lone meeting (the UK-Kansas game of December 16, 1950) and eventually passed Allen on the all-time wins list for college coaches. Rupp retired after the 1971-72 season as college basketball's winningest coach, a distinction he later lost to North Carolina's Dean Smith, another Allen disciple.

Before Rupp took over at Kentucky in the fall of 1930, the Wildcats had enjoyed a modicum of success. But Rupp arrival's from the Illinois high school ranks signaled an instant ascent to the upper reaches of Southern basketball and, eventually, a prominent place on the national stage. Using a fast-break system that emphasized quick, crisp passing, Rupp's teams stormed through the Southeastern Conference (a league founded in 1932-33, with lineage tracing to the old Southern Intercollegiate Athletic Association and the Southern Conference). By the mid-1940s, Kentucky was ready for bigger things.

The first breakthrough came in 1946, when the Wildcats finished 28-2 and won the NIT by defeating Rhode Island in the title game at Madison Square Garden. Two years later, UK was on top of the basketball world. It won the SEC Tournament title and the NCAA crown, then teamed with the AAU champion Phillips Oilers and four other standout players to rip through all comers in the Olympics. This Kentucky team, known as the Fabulous Five, boasted some of UK's legendary names—Alex Groza, Ralph Beard and Wallace "Wah Wah" Jones. It scaled the first peak in a mountainous dynasty that established the Wildcats as the nation's premier basketball program.

There were some who believed Kentucky was mostly fattening up on its football-mad SEC rivals, beating severely undermanned teams that were playing in dinky gyms with tiny budgets. It was true that Rupp's teams held a mastery over the conference that never would be replicated—they won their first

Adolph Rupp had plenty of superior talent on hand (left to right, Cliff Hagan, Lou Tsioropoulos and Frank Ramsey) to execute what he had drawn up on the blackboard.

30 SEC regular-season games (1933-35) and later won 92 of 94 regular-season games from the 1945-46 season through the 1953-54 season. But the Cats extended their mastery to the rest of the country, particularly from 1945-46 through 1950-51, when Kentucky captured three national championships and that NIT title while compiling a 187-12 record. It was a tremendous chapter in college basketball history, and Rupp wrote it with teams that matched his undying commitment to detail and perfection. They ran and defended to the death. They were rarely complacent. And they kept winning.

But the good times came crashing down when Rupp's program was suspended for the 1952-53 season, because of the involvement of UK players in a nationwide point-shaving scandal from 1948 through 1951 and SEC allegations that some players received illegal financial inducements. Though Rupp appeared to have no knowledge of his players' associations with gamblers and

> *Rupp was a complex man. He was sarcastic and demanding of his players. He was hardheaded and too proud.*

other unsavory characters, it all happened on his watch.

Whatever pent-up frustration the '52-'53 team might have felt—players on that squad were forced to sit out the season because of the transgressions of others—it was unleashed the following season, when the Wildcats returned to competition and blitzed the field. But despite a 25-0 record and a No. 1 ranking in the Associated Press' poll, Kentucky declined a berth in the NCAA Tournament when the NCAA ruled that UK stars Cliff Hagan, Frank Ramsey and Lou Tsioropoulos were ineligible because of their status as graduate students. Though the remaining players voted to play in the tourney, Rupp wouldn't allow it—he didn't want to risk the perfect season with a team made up predominantly of reserves.

Rupp's teams reached the regional finals in the NCAA tourney in 1956 and 1957 but were foiled in their attempts to reach the Final Four. But after losing six regular-season games in 1957-58, the Wildcats caught fire in postseason play and went on to capture their fourth NCAA crown under Rupp. The Fiddlin' Five escaped Temple in the national semifinals, 61-60, and whipped Elgin Baylor and Seattle, 84-72, in the title game. That was the last championship Rupp would win. The 1966 all-white Rupp's Runts made it to the final game but were defeated by a Texas Western team that started five black players. It was a game that many used as fodder in their arguments against Rupp the man. His reluctance to buck the SEC's historic refusal to recruit black players was on full display against Texas Western, and he and his team paid a price. So, too, did other mid-1960s coaches and schools found lagging in race relations.

In the final analysis, Rupp was a complex man. He was sarcastic and demanding of his players. He was hardheaded and too proud, as he proved when he fought the state's mandatory retirement age—and lost. But he was a giant on the basketball court, and his accomplishments and stewardship made Kentucky basketball what it is today.

joe b. hall

How do you follow a legend? Well, you need some thick skin, because even if you capture a national championship and win nearly 75 percent of your games, you still might not measure up.

Joe B. Hall, who coached Kentucky to a 297-100 record (.748 winning percentage) over 13 seasons and directed the Wildcats to the 1978 NCAA title, grew up a UK fan, played at Kentucky and was an assistant coach under Adolph Rupp. Yet that background couldn't prepare him for the pressure and expectations that came from following Rupp, a larger-than-life figure.

But for all of the shiny items on his resume, Hall wasn't Rupp, and that made his life difficult in Lexington.

Hall played sparingly in his one season of varsity basketball at Kentucky and finished his collegiate eligibility at the University of the South. After serving as a high school coach and then getting college-level experience with five seasons at Regis (Colo.) and one at Central Missouri State, he joined Rupp's staff for the 1965-66 season. After the 1971-72 season, when Rupp retired after 41 seasons on the bench and 876 wins, Hall was a logical successor. He also was a successful one. But for all of the shiny items on his resume, Hall wasn't Rupp, and that made his life difficult in Lexington.

It didn't help much that Hall's second team finished 13-13, only the second time in 47 years that Kentucky had failed to win more games than it lost. The Wildcats made quick amends, reaching the national championship game in 1975, Hall's third season, before losing to UCLA in coach John Wooden's final game. UK's 1976 NIT title was a nice consolation prize, but it was the 1977-78 season that gave Hall and his supporters some real ammunition. With Jack Givens providing the firepower, Kyle Macy the stewardship and Rick Robey, Mike Phillips and James Lee the muscle, Kentucky rolled to 30 wins and the national championship.

Kentucky didn't win another NCAA crown under Hall, but it did reach the 1984 Final Four. In Hall's final season, Kentucky struggled to a 16-12 regular-season mark before reaching the Sweet Sixteen in the 1985 NCAA Tournament.

In addition to the national championship, Hall's legacy includes a much more liberal approach to recruiting. Under Hall, Kentucky welcomed unprecedented numbers of black athletes, a policy that helped UK remain a national power.

Adolph Rupp was a tough act to follow, but Joe B. Hall led the Wildcats to their first NCAA championship in two decades (opposite page). Under Hall's leadership, Kentucky recruited an unprecedented number of black players—a move that bolstered UK's image and also helped it remain a national power.

eddie sutton

Eddie Sutton arrived in Lexington with impressive credentials. He had led Arkansas to nine consecutive NCAA Tournament appearances and had taken the Razorbacks to the 1978 Final Four. It was a tremendous accomplishment for a school that had made only four previous trips to the tourney. And though he didn't have a Kentucky pedigree, Sutton was thought to be a good successor to Joe B. Hall, thanks to his strong commitment to defense.

His hiring at Kentucky was seen as a strong next step for the university.

Born in Kansas, Sutton was a guard on the 1958 Oklahoma State team that advanced to the Elite Eight of the NCAA Tournament. He began his coaching career at his alma mater as a graduate assistant to the great Hank Iba. After head-coaching stints in the high school and junior college ranks, Sutton took over the Creighton program in the fall of 1969. After five seasons, he moved on to Arkansas, where his teams won 260 games over 11 seasons. His hiring at Kentucky was seen as a strong next step for the university.

Things didn't turn out that way. Sutton lasted four seasons in Lexington and left with the program in serious trouble. Not that things didn't begin well in 1985-86. With Sutton earning national coach-of-the-year honors, the Wildcats posted a 32-4 record in his first season and won the SEC championship with a 17-1 mark. Top-seeded UK marched to the Southeast Regional final in the NCAA Tournament, but the Wildcats were stunned, 59-57, by LSU, an 11th seed that earlier in the season had lost to UK three times.

The 1986-87 season was a tough one for Sutton. Injuries plagued Kentucky throughout—at one point, only seven scholarship players were available. The result was an 18-11 record, a third-place SEC finish and a first-round exit from the NCAA Tournament. Those memories were erased in 1987-88 when the Wildcats bolted to a 10-0 start. Although the Cats went on to lose five SEC games, they won both the regular-season and conference tourney titles. But after two NCAA tourney victories, Kentucky fell to Villanova in the Southeast semifinals.

Then came the avalanche. With NCAA investigators at the door, Kentucky staggered to a 13-19 record in 1988-89, the school's first losing season since 1926-27. In May 1989, the UK program was put on probation for three years because of recruiting and academic violations, the sanctions decreasing scholarships, limiting television exposure and forcing the Cats to surrender their 1988 SEC titles and NCAA victories. It was a dark time for Kentucky basketball and the end of Sutton's reign in Lexington.

In his first season at Kentucky, Eddie Sutton guided the Cats to a 32-4 record. Before long, though, he and the UK program were immersed in big trouble.

rick pitino

In some ways, there couldn't have been a more incongruous choice to revitalize the ailing Kentucky program than Rick Pitino. The fast-talking Pitino had no connection whatsoever to Kentucky basketball or the Bluegrass State. But there was no doubting his track record, and few could deny his passion or commitment to making the Wildcats great again. Kentucky fans may have had trouble understanding the Easterner's accent, and many of the colorful characters who orbited Planet Pitino weren't quite the usual UK types, but once the Wildcats started winning, Pitino might as well have been born and bred in Owensboro.

Pitino moved back to the college game to direct what he referred to, only half-jokingly, as basketball's "Holy Roman Empire."

Pitino first gained national prominence by taking Providence to the Final Four in 1987. The Friars' on-court personality resembled that of their brash coach. They pressed relentlessly and shot 3-pointers in bunches. From there, Pitino moved to the New York Knicks, whom he lifted from NBA mediocrity to the 1989 Atlantic Division title. Kentucky came calling after that, and Pitino moved back to the college game to direct what he referred to, only half-jokingly, as basketball's "Holy Roman Empire."

Of course, there was plenty of work to do. The Wildcats were reeling from NCAA sanctions and had little hope of competing for the SEC title, much less recapturing national glory anytime soon. So, Pitino focused on creating excitement. His first squad in 1989-90 finished 14-14, but those Wildcats put up 3-point attempts from all over the court and played with heart and enthusiasm. It was all gravy from there. In 1990-91, Kentucky finished 22-6 and closed the year ranked ninth in the Associated Press' poll. Though UK was still banned from NCAA Tournament play, it was clear that the Wildcats and their new coach were on a remarkable upswing— one that culminated in a memorable 1991-92 season. That Kentucky team, dubbed "The Unforgettables," won the SEC East title, the conference tournament and three NCAA tourney games before losing to Duke, 104-103, in the East Regional final. The Duke-UK thriller is considered by many the greatest college basketball game ever played.

Pitino's 1992-93 Wildcats advanced to the Final Four. Then, three years later, Kentucky won its first national championship in 18 years when it conquered Syracuse, 76-67, in the Jersey Meadowlands, just across the Hudson River from Pitino's native New York. Though Pitino failed the next year in an attempt to lead Kentucky to back-to-back national titles— UK lost to Arizona in overtime in the NCAA final—few can dispute his lofty place in Kentucky basketball history.

At the start of his reign in Lexington, Rick Pitino restored excitement and pride. His next big task was building a championship team—and he succeeded.

tubby smith

If Rick Pitino's selection as the man to follow Eddie Sutton at Kentucky appeared somewhat odd, considering Pitino's Eastern roots and slick persona, then the decision to turn the program over to Tubby Smith when Pitino returned to the NBA was even more curious—not to mention groundbreaking.

Thirty years before, Kentucky was unwilling to recruit black players and perceived by many as almost militant in its decision not to do so. Now, in 1997-98, the Wildcats would be led by a black coach. For the first year or so of his tenure, Smith endured countless interviews about the color of his skin, rather than the prestige of his resume. It was big news, but after a while, the issue went away.

It didn't hurt that Smith won the national championship in his first season at Kentucky. At that point, his skin could have been plaid and Wildcat Nation wouldn't have cared. Smith cut down the nets after the last game. That was the main thing.

For the first year or so of his tenure, Smith endured countless interviews about the color of his skin, rather than the prestige of his resume.

Orlando Smith attended high school in Maryland and graduated from High Point (N.C.) University, where he was a four-year letterman in basketball. He spent six years as a high school coach before serving as an assistant on the staffs at Virginia Commonwealth, South Carolina and, in 1989-90 and 1990-91, Kentucky. He was part of Pitino's dream staff that included future head coaches Ralph Willard, Billy Donovan and Herb Sendek. Those two years at UK made Smith a hot commodity, and he moved on to direct the Tulsa program in 1991-92.

Four seasons and two Sweet Sixteen appearances later, Smith was even in more demand. He accepted the top spot at Georgia and posted a 45-19 mark in two seasons at Athens, including another Sweet Sixteen berth. When the Wildcats needed a new coach after the 1996-97 season, Smith was the only man interviewed for the job. And he delivered.

The obvious highlight of Smith's first season at Kentucky was an improbable NCAA Tournament run that included come-from-behind victories in each of the Wildcats' final three games. The Cats made up a 17-point second-half deficit in the South Regional final against Duke, climbed out of a 10-point hole in the second half of the national semifinals against Stanford and then used relentless defensive pressure to overcome the largest halftime deficit (10 points) in title-game history and upend Utah.

Smith has won three SEC Tournament titles during his five years at Kentucky and also taken the Wildcats to the Elite Eight (1999) and Sweet Sixteen (2001, 2002).

An ever-focused Tubby Smith had good reason to exult in his first season as Wildcats coach—he led Kentucky on a stirring run to the 1998 NCAA crown.

Cats Legends

First Team

dan issel

no. 44   **ht:** 6'8"   **wt:** 240   **pos:** center

hometown: batavia, illinois

seasons: 1968, 1969, 1970

If you want sheer production, Issel is your man. He is Kentucky's all-time leading scorer with 2,138 points—despite playing only three seasons. His school records include most points scored in one game (53) and one season (948) and highest career scoring average (25.8). Issel also is UK's career leader in rebounds (1,078). A bruising interior player, he sometimes lags behind on the UK honor roll because he didn't play on a national championship team. But if high-scoring guard Mike Casey hadn't missed the 1969-70 season (because of injuries suffered in car crash), the Wildcats might well have challenged UCLA for the national title that year. Issel made an immediate impact in 1967-68, scoring 18 points against Michigan in his UK debut and averaging 16.4 points overall. In the '68 NCAA Mideast Regional, he had 36 points and 13 rebounds against Marquette. Issel excelled as a junior, finishing with a 26.6 scoring average. He had a remarkable game against LSU that season, punishing the Tigers with 36 points and 29 rebounds. As a senior in '69-'70, Issel was clearly the Wildcats' main scoring option, and he responded with a consensus All-American season that featured a 33.9-point average, a 53-point spree against Mississippi and a 51-point performance vs. LSU. In Kentucky's NCAA Tournament win over Notre Dame, he scored 44 points, which helped offset Austin Carr's 52 for the Fighting Irish. Issel also had point totals of 47, 43, 41 and 40 (twice) in his final season, which ended one game short of the Final Four when Jacksonville stopped UK, 106-100, in the Mideast Regional title game. Issel outscored Artis Gilmore, his future pro teammate, 28-24, in that game.

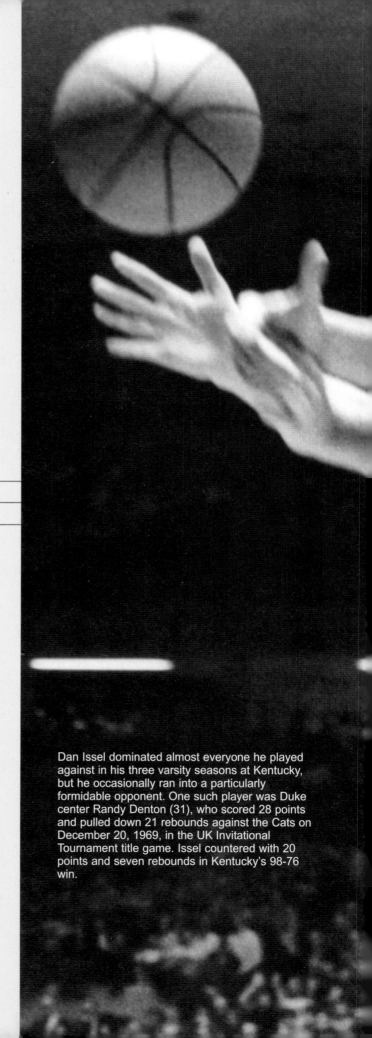

Dan Issel dominated almost everyone he played against in his three varsity seasons at Kentucky, but he occasionally ran into a particularly formidable opponent. One such player was Duke center Randy Denton (31), who scored 28 points and pulled down 21 rebounds against the Cats on December 20, 1969, in the UK Invitational Tournament title game. Issel countered with 20 points and seven rebounds in Kentucky's 98-76 win.

First Team

ralph beard

no. 12 **ht:** 5'10" **wt:** 175 **pos:** guard

hometown: louisville, kentucky

seasons: 1946, 1947, 1948, 1949

Perhaps the most fabulous member of the Fabulous Five—he was a three-time consensus All-American—Beard was a backcourt marvel and Kentucky's on-court leader during the most prosperous period in the Wildcats' grand basketball history. With Beard at the point, the Wildcats won their first two NCAA championships (1948, 1949), captured an NIT title (1946) and combined with the Phillips Oilers AAU team to win Olympic gold ('48). Beard, from Louisville (Male High School), came to Kentucky bent on playing football and basketball. But a shoulder injury early in his days as a UK halfback ended his football career, and Beard soon was focusing all of his energies on the hardwood—and maximizing his substantial skills. Extremely quick off the dribble and relentless on the defensive end, Beard often overwhelmed opponents. He sparked the Wildcats' pressure tactics at both ends of the floor, forcing turnovers and turning them into easy buckets. Though not a great scorer, Beard nonetheless finished his career with 1,517 points, good for 13th on Kentucky's all-time list, and as a sophomore he led UK's 1947 NIT runner-up team in scoring with a 10.9 average. He hit the winning free throw against Rhode Island in the 1946 NIT title game. Beard scored a career-high 12.5 points per game in 1947-48, and he was the second-leading scorer in that season's NCAA championship game (12 points against Baylor). Although implicated in the gambling scandals of the early 1950s, Beard remains a Kentucky hero.

Backcourt marvel Ralph Beard, on his way to a 13-point game, drove past Bob Curran of Holy Cross in the Eastern final of the 1948 NCAA Tournament, a game in which Kentucky prevailed by a 60-52 score. The triumph at New York's Madison Square Garden moved Beard and the Wildcats within one victory of UK's first NCAA championship. Beard was extremely quick off the dribble and a tenacious defender while wearing the blue and white.

First Team

cliff hagan

As teammate Frank Ramsey watched from afar, Cliff Hagan battled LSU players under the basket in the 1952 SEC Tournament final. Hagan scored 19 points in the Wildcats' 44-43 victory over the Tigers. It was a typical performance by Hagan, who was winding down a season in which he averaged 21.6 points and 16.5 rebounds. The Owensboro, Ky., product was a superior hook-shot artist and a force on the backboards.

no. 6   **ht:** 6'4"   **wt:** 200   **pos:** forward/center

hometown: owensboro, kentucky

seasons: 1951, 1952, 1954

Hagan was a legendary Kentucky high school player who continued his basketball exploits in Lexington and then in the NBA. Though only 6-4, he was a dominant frontcourt player capable of burning opponents with his hook shot or humbling them on the backboards. By the time Hagan was done at UK, he had played on a national championship team that finished 32-2 and starred on a 25-0 team. Hagan remains one of the four or five best Kentucky prep performers ever, yet he wasn't an immediate star at UK. He appeared in only 20 games as a sophomore in 1950-51 but did average 9.2 points that season for a Wildcats team that won the NCAA crown. In the title game against Kansas State, Hagan shook off a throat infection and helped rally the Cats to victory (he scored 10 points overall). There was no stopping Hagan as a junior. He took over at center at the outset of the 1951-52 season when Bill Spivey was sidelined because of knee problems and led the Cats with a 21.6 scoring average and 16.5 rebounds per game (the third-highest season rebound average in school history). The remarkable performance earned Hagan consensus All-American honors. He and Frank Ramsey were a lethal pair that season, sparking UK to a 29-3 record. Hagan was in top form in his final season, 1953-54, showing no effects from the one-year suspension of the Kentucky program. He led Kentucky with a 24-point average and 13.5 rebounds per game, again winning consensus All-American designation. The Wildcats rolled to an undefeated season, but Hagan, Ramsey and Lou Tsioropoulos were declared ineligible for the NCAA Tournament because of their fifth-year status.

First Team

jamal mashburn

The Wildcats' Jamal Mashburn mashed more than a few of his opponents, displaying a rare combination of outside firepower and interior muscle. He stepped up as a sophomore, supplying the big-star qualities that turned UK's band of Unforgettables into a truly unforgettable team. As a junior, the New Yorker sparked Kentucky to the Final Four and won consensus All-American honors. A somewhat placid demeanor belied Mashburn's ability to take control on the court.

no. 24   **height:** 6'8"   **wt:** 240   **pos:** forward

hometown: bronx, new york

seasons: 1991, 1992, 1993

If there were any doubts whether Rick Pitino could turn around the Wildcats in the post-probation days, they disappeared in the fall of 1990 when Mashburn arrived on campus. Not only was the 6-8 Mashburn a highly talented wing, he was from the Bronx. That Pitino was able to grab a prep All-American out of his native New York at a time when the Kentucky program was reeling demonstrated the coach's ability to sell his vision beyond Wildcat Nation. Mashburn was a rare combination of outside firepower and interior muscle. Nicknamed "Monster Mash" for his ability to dominate opponents close to the basket, Mashburn was a soft-spoken collegian with a wide smile and a somewhat placid demeanor on the court. But there was nothing polite about his ability to fill a stat sheet. He averaged 12.9 points as a freshman for a surprising 22-6 team that began the Pitino-era resurgence. He asserted himself as a sophomore in 1991-92, leading the Wildcats in scoring with a 21.3 average and in rebounding with a 7.8 mark. He converted 56.7 percent of his field-goal tries and 43.9 percent of his 3-point attempts, both team-leading figures. Most important, he brought mega-star skills to a starting unit featuring plucky seniors known as the Unforgettables. He was outstanding in Kentucky's NCAA Tournament run, scoring 27 points against Iowa State and 30 vs. Massachusetts. In the agonizing 104-103 overtime loss to Duke in the East Regional final, he finished with 28 points. As a junior, Mashburn averaged 21 points, led the Wildcats to the Final Four and earned consensus All-American honors. He then declared for the NBA draft.

First Team

kyle macy

Kyle Macy knew when to pass and when to shoot—and he did both with consummate skill. He led Kentucky in assists three times and finished with career shooting percentages of .521 from the field and .890 from the free-throw line (the latter a school record). One of the most popular players in UK history, Macy was a stabilizing force as a sophomore on the 1978 national champs and a consensus All-American two years later.

no. 4 **ht:** 6'3" **wt:** 180 **position:** guard

hometown: peru, indiana

seasons: 1978, 1979, 1980

No. 4 looked like a choirboy—from his usually neat haircut all the way down to his socks, on which he always dried his hands before shooting free throws. But Macy was a resolute leader on the court, and his countenance belied his determination and ability to perform in pressure situations. An import from both the Indiana high school ranks and Purdue (he transferred from the Big Ten university to Lexington after one year), he became one of the most popular Wildcats of all time. It didn't hurt that as a sophomore he was the stabilizing force on Kentucky's 1978 national title team—those Cats finished 30-2—or that as a senior he was a consensus All-American. A three-time UK assists leader who scored 1,411 career points, Macy was a savvy point man who knew when to pass and when to shoot. He scored 12.5 points per game in his first UK season and established himself as a deadly free-throw shooter. His 10 made foul shots in 11 attempts (and 18 points overall) proved crucial in the 1978 Mideast Regional final victory over Michigan State. In the '78 NCAA championship game against Duke, Macy scored nine points and handed out eight assists. Kentucky slumped to a 19-12 record in 1978-79, but Macy posted a team-high 15.2 scoring average. As a senior in 1979-80, he led the 29-6 Wildcats with 15.4 points per game and, in addition to his All-American honors, was named Player of the Year in the Southeastern Conference. His .890 career free-throw percentage remains a UK record.

Second Team

jack givens

Jack Givens had many notable accomplishments in his four years in Lexington—as his No. 3 ranking on the Wildcats' all-time scoring list would suggest. But the Goose will forever be remembered in UK lore because of his sensational performance against Duke in the 1978 NCAA title game. In his final appearance in a Cats uniform, he torched the Blue Devils for 41 points. Givens finished his UK career with 2,038 points and 793 rebounds.

no. 21 **ht:** 6'4" **wt:** 205 **pos:** forward

hometown: lexington, kentucky

seasons: 1975, 1976, 1977, 1978

Givens ranks third on Kentucky's all-time scoring list with 2,038 points. He led the Wildcats in scoring three consecutive seasons. His .553 field-goal percentage as a senior is noteworthy, and his career .798 free-throw accuracy stands out. His 793 career rebounds also are impressive. But any discussion of the Goose must commence with one number: 41. That's how many points Givens scored against Duke in the 1978 NCAA championship game, and his amazing production lifted the Wildcats to their fifth national crown. In his 37 minutes of action, Givens was unstoppable in a performance that gave Joe B. Hall the title he needed to legitimize his standing as a worthy successor to Adolph Rupp. Givens' career wasn't all about one game, of course. He averaged 9.4 points as a freshman forward on Kentucky's 1975 national runner-up team, and the Lexington native scored a game-high 24 in UK's Final Four victory over Syracuse. Givens averaged a team-high 20.1 points the next season for a Kentucky team that won the NIT championship, and the Goose led the way again in 1976-77 with an 18.9 scoring average. The Wildcats came within one win of the 1977 Final Four; in the loss that denied them the trip, Givens had 26 points against North Carolina in the East Regional final. UK's disappointments in 1975 and 1977 gave way to ecstasy in 1978. With Givens (18.1-point average) leading a deep and hugely talented team, Kentucky scored 90 or more points 14 times and rampaged to a 30-2 record. And when it came down to the final game against a young and feisty Duke team, Givens wasn't to be denied. The Goose soared, and so did Kentucky.

Second Team

frank ramsey

no. 30   **ht:** 6'3"   **wt:** 185   **pos:** guard

hometown: madisonville, kentucky

seasons: 1951, 1952, 1954

If there is any question about Ramsey's commitment to winning, it can be answered with the statistic that shows the 6-3 Kentucky native with 1,038 career rebounds—a total that ranks second to Dan Issel's 1,078 in UK history. Ramsey wasn't a great outside shooter, but few could deny him off the dribble. He was a strong defender and a consummate team player. Those qualities served him well later as a member of the powerful Boston Celtics, the NBA's ultimate collection of unselfish performers. Ramsey was a sophomore member of Kentucky's 1951 national championship team, and he averaged 10.1 points and 12.8 rebounds that season. In the NCAA Tournament, he scored 14 points against Louisville and a team-high 13 in a triumph over St. John's. He also had 12 rebounds against Illinois. But Ramsey's true fame came in his final two UK seasons, when he teamed with Cliff Hagan to form a potent scoring tandem. As a junior in 1951-52, Ramsey scored 15.9 points per game and averaged 12 rebounds for a Kentucky team that won 29 of 32 games. Those Wildcats appeared a threat for a second consecutive national crown before losing Bill Spivey, who missed the early part of the schedule because of a knee injury and then sat out the remainder of the season because of an ongoing NCAA investigation into the point-shaving scandal that had rocked college basketball. After UK basketball was mothballed for one season, Ramsey scored at a 19.6 clip in 1953-54 and helped the Cats to a 25-0 season. He had a 37-point game against Tennessee and got 30 points against LSU in the final game of his UK career.

Frank Ramsey wasn't a gifted long-range marksman, but few could deny him off the dribble. A fierce competitor, he ranks second on the Cats' career rebounds list despite standing only 6-3. Ramsey averaged 10.1 points and 12.8 rebounds for UK's 1951 national champs. After the Kentucky program was shut down in 1952-53, Ramsey came back to score at a 19.6 clip the following season.

Second Team

louie dampier

A 6-footer, Louie Dampier was the runt of the litter on the undersized 1965-66 Wildcats. Yet he was one of the most talented players on Rupp's Runts— and the best pure shooter in the storied history of Kentucky basketball. Time and again, Dampier let fly from far out in the pre-3-point-shot era. Still, he knocked down 50.8 percent of his field-goal attempts. He averaged 21.1 points for UK's national runner-up team of '66.

no. 10   **ht:** 6'0"   **wt:** 167   **pos:** guard

hometown: indianapolis, indiana

seasons: 1965, 1966, 1967

The greatest pure shooter in Kentucky history, Dampier would have been danger personified had he played college ball in the era of the 3-point field goal. Not that he wasn't a force in his three varsity years in Lexington. Dampier finished with 1,575 points, good for 11th place on the all-time Wildcats list. What's particularly remarkable is his career .508 field-goal percentage, considering how many of his shots were put up from long range. Dampier scored 18 points against Iowa in his UK debut and finished with a team-high 17-point average in his first season (1964-65), but the Wildcats managed only a 15-10 record and wound up fifth in the SEC. Kentucky's fortunes changed dramatically the next year, when Rupp's Runts compiled a 27-2 record and reached the NCAA title game. Dampier again was a big gun, averaging 21.1 points overall (second to Pat Riley's 22-point figure) and playing standout ball in the 1966 NCAA Tournament. In the Mideast Regional, the 6-foot guard torched Dayton for 34 points, making 14 of 23 floor shots, and he scored 15 against Michigan. In the national semifinals, he poured in a team-high 23 in UK's triumph over Duke. In the title game against Texas Western, Dampier scored 19 points but was held to 7-of-18 shooting by the victorious Miners. Amazingly, Dampier led Kentucky with nine rebounds. Although Kentucky faltered to a 13-13 record in 1966-67—its worst-ever mark under Adolph Rupp—Dampier scored a UK-leading 20.6 points per game and scored 30 or more points six times. He then became an American Basketball Association legend with the Kentucky Colonels, making the most of the league's 3-point shot and finishing as the league's all-time leading scorer.

Second Team

kenny walker

no. 34   **ht:** 6'8"   **wt:** 190   **pos:** forward

hometown: roberta, georgia

seasons: 1983, 1984, 1985, 1986

Tall, quick and spectacular, Walker began his Kentucky career slowly but enjoyed two banner seasons that vaulted him among the elite Wildcats of all time. Recruited out of Georgia, Walker is a prime example of how coach Joe B. Hall aggressively integrated the Kentucky program and made it attractive for standout players from around the country. Walker averaged a modest 7.3 points as a freshman, although he did enjoy considerable prosperity late in the season and became a major part of the rotation when the 1983 NCAA Tournament rolled around. He scored 13 points against Indiana in the Mideast Regional—but that was just an appetizer. Walker then played a key role on Kentucky's 1984 Final Four entry, finishing second on the team in scoring (12.4 average) and reaching double-figure point totals in 15 consecutive games. "Sky" Walker took over in 1984-85, leading the Cats in scoring, field-goal percentage, free-throw accuracy, rebounding and blocked shots. His figure of 22.9 points per game not only led UK, it made Walker the only Wildcat to average in double digits. With Walker out in front, Kentucky shrugged off a mediocre regular season to win two games in the 1985 NCAA tourney. In one of the victories, against Washington, he had 29 points and 10 rebounds. As a senior in 1985-86, Walker was a consensus All-American. He maintained his statistical dominance and on-court leadership and helped Eddie Sutton's first UK team win 32 games and a berth in the Elite Eight. Walker, who averaged 20 points in his final season, is Kentucky's No. 2 career scorer with 2,080 points.

The sky was the limit for Kenny Walker, a bundle of talent from Georgia who averaged only 7.3 points as a Wildcats freshman but seemed destined for greatness. Walker realized that greatness, winding up as the second-leading scorer in Kentucky history with 2,080 points. In 1983-84, the man called "Sky" was a key player on UK's Final Four team, averaging 12.4 points, and the next two seasons he scored a team-leading 22.9 and 20 points per game.

alex groza

no. 15   **ht:** 6'7"   **wt:** 220   **pos:** center

hometown: martins ferry, ohio

seasons: 1945, 1947, 1948, 1949

Even though a stint in the military interrupted his career, and involvement in a point-shaving scandal tainted his legend to some degree, Groza still ranks as one of Kentucky's all-time greats. He was the man in the middle on two national championship teams and a standout for three-plus seasons. Groza showed potential greatness by averaging 16.5 points in 10 games as a freshman in 1944-45, but at that juncture he left UK for the service and didn't return until the fall of 1946. He became the perfect center for Adolph Rupp's fast, quick-passing system. Strong enough to handle opposing centers, Groza also possessed quickness and the good hands necessary to shine in Rupp's system. With Ralph Beard scoring 10.9 points per game and Groza averaging 10.6, the 1946-47 Wildcats won 34 games but fell to Utah in the NIT championship game. Groza and Beard then shared the UK scoring lead with 12.5 averages in 1947-48, leading the Fabulous Five to 36 wins and Kentucky's first-ever NCAA title. Groza scored a game-high 14 points as the Cats defeated Baylor for the championship. He was the No. 1 scorer on the 1948 U.S. Olympic gold-medal team, averaged 11.1 points. Groza was even more impressive in 1948-49, scoring a UK-best 20.5 points per game and leading the Wildcats to another national crown. He was unstoppable in the NCAA Tournament, scoring 30 points against Villanova, 27 vs. Illinois and 25 of Kentucky's 46 points in the title game against Oklahoma A&M. Groza finished his Wildcats career with 1,744 points, a total that is ninth on the school's all-time list. He was a two-time consensus All-Amercian.

Alex Groza (No. 15) was the perfect man in the middle for Adolph Rupp's fast-paced style of play, possessing quickness, good hands and the ability to dominate inside. The Ohioan helped the Cats to back-to-back national titles, proving virtually unstoppable in the 1949 NCAA Tournament with 82 points in three games. In Groza's three full seasons in a Kentucky uniform, the Cats won 102 of 110 games. As a senior, he averaged 20.5 points.

Third Team

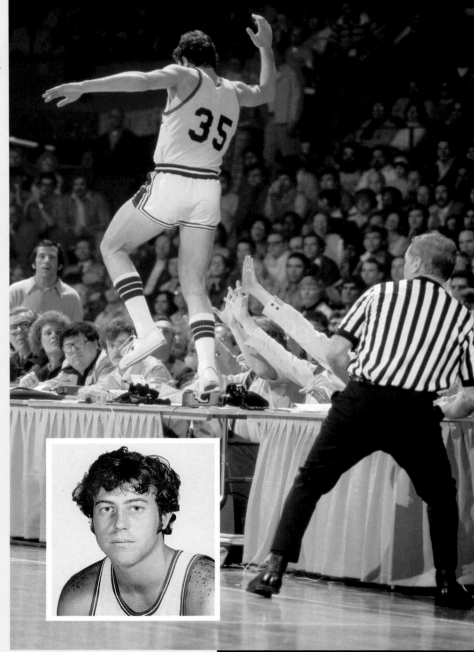

kevin grevey

no. 35   **ht:** 6'5"   **wt:** 205

pos: guard/forward

hometown: hamilton, ohio

seasons: 1973, 1974, 1975

A tricky lefthander who excelled at shaking defenders and scoring in many ways from a variety of spots on the floor, Grevey sparked the Wildcats' run to the 1975 NCAA championship game. Grevey was Mr. Basketball in Ohio, but he answered Adolph Rupp's call to play for the Wildcats. He never did play for the Baron, though. Rupp's last season at UK, 1971-72, was Grevey's first—and freshmen weren't eligible for varsity competition. Grevey scored only six points in his first game as a Wildcat, but he soon settled in as a productive sophomore in 1972-73 under new coach Joe B. Hall. Grevey scored 18.7 points per game that season—the second-best figure on the team—and showed fans what was ahead with several big performances, including a 40-point outburst against Georgia. He was The Man in 1973-74 with a 21.9 scoring average, even though the Wildcats struggled to a 13-13 record. He had 25 or more points 11 times but often lacked the support needed to lift the Cats to victory. Most of the frustration from that un-Kentucky-like season was wiped away in Grevey's senior year, when the Wildcats fashioned a 26-5 record, shared the SEC title and went on a thrilling NCAA run that ended with a loss to UCLA in coach John Wooden's final game. Grevey scored 34 points against the Bruins in the title game, capping a season in which he averaged 23.6 points and a career in which he scored 1,801 points.

bill spivey

no. 77   **ht:** 7'0"   **wt:** 230   **pos:** center   **hometown:** warner robins, georgia   **seasons:** 1950, 1951

Had Spivey not been so loyal to his teammates, he might have won lasting basketball fame. But Spivey was part of the collateral damage of the point-shaving scandal that shook the Kentucky program, even though he never accepted a bribe or consorted with unsavory figures. His crimes were being offered money but not reporting it and knowing his friends' roles in the sordid affair but being unwilling to turn them in. Besides losing his senior season at Kentucky, Spivey was banned from the NBA. The 7-foot Spivey had been an immediate sensation in Lexington, averaging 19.3 points as sophomore in 1949-50, setting a Kentucky record (broken many times since) with a 40-point game and helping UK to a 25-5 record. In 1950-51, he averaged 19.2 points and 17.2 rebounds (the second-best mark in UK history) and helped power the Cats to a 32-2 record and the NCAA championship. Spivey won consensus All-American honors that season, and he helped Adolph Rupp defeat Phog Allen, the Kentucky coach's mentor at Kansas. In a 68-39 romp, Spivey outscored Jayhawks star Clyde Lovellette, 22-10. In the '51 national title game, he overwhelmed Kansas State with a monster outing of 22 points and 21 rebounds. That was it for Spivey, who was sidelined early in his senior season because of a knee injury and wound up not playing at all when he volunteered to sit out until he was cleared of any wrongdoing in the scandal. Eventually, the UK Athletics Board suspended his eligibility.

tony delk

no. 00 **ht:** 6'1" **wt:** 193 **pos:** guard
hometown: brownsville, tennessee
seasons: 1993, 1994, 1995, 1996

Delk had long, vine-like arms and a deadly shooting eye. A high scorer as a prep player in Tennessee, he was immediately turned into a point guard when Rick Pitino reasoned that a 6-1 player shouldn't be on the wing. Wrong move. Delk struggled in his first season at UK but thrived in the next three, when he earned time at the two spot. He was a freshman role player on the Wildcats' 1993 Final Four team, backing up Travis Ford at the point and hitting an occasional 3-pointer. Taking over the shooting-guard position in 1993-94, Delk led the Wildcats in scoring (16.6 average) and sank a team-high 95 3-pointers, the third-best season total in Kentucky history. He again led the Wildcats in scoring in 1994-95, averaging 16.7 points. He got 76 points in four NCAA tourney games that season, his top effort being a 26-point outing against Arizona State. Delk then posted a career-high 17.8 scoring average as a UK senior and led the Wildcats to their sixth national crown. Sure, he had his regular-season moments—he made a school-record nine 3-pointers against Texas Christian—but his play in the 1996 NCAA Tournament was a cut above. Delk scored 20 or more points in four of Kentucky's six tourney games, and he tied an NCAA championship game record with seven 3-pointers against Syracuse. He was a consensus All-American in '96. Delk ended his career with 1,890 points (fourth-best in Kentucky history) and a UK-record 283 3-pointers.

wah wah jones

no. 27 **ht:** 6'4" **wt:** 205 **position:** forward
hometown: harlan, kentucky
seasons: 1946, 1947, 1948, 1949

Jones could have excelled in just about any sport—that's how talented he was. Big, tough and fearless, he came from the coal country of Harlan, Ky., where he was a schoolboy legend. A four-year letterman in both basketball and football at UK, Jones was a key player on Kentucky basketball teams that won 130 of 140 games, captured back-to-back NCAA championships, took one NIT title and had a second-place NIT finish. Jones was not an accomplished scorer but nonetheless wound up his career with 1,151 points. "Wah Wah"—when Jones was young, his given name Wallace was mispronounced—was an interior stalwart who could rebound, defend and score when needed. Though 6-4, he played the power positions for Adolph Rupp's team but also possessed the quickness to operate in the open court. As a freshman, Jones averaged 9.7 points for UK's 1946 NIT champions. He slumped to a 5.9 mark as sophomore—due in part to injuries—as Kentucky went 34-3 but lost to Utah in the NIT final. In 1947-48, Jones was the No. 3 scorer (9.3) on the Fabulous Five and stood out in the NCAA Tournament. He scored 21 points against Columbia and got nine as part of UK's balanced attack in the triumph over Baylor for the national title. Jones scored 8.6 points per game as a senior in 1948-49, won All-Southeastern Conference designation for the fourth consecutive season and played rock-solid defense for a Kentucky team that repeated as NCAA champions.

cotton nash

no. 44 **ht:** 6'5" **wt:** 220 **pos:** forward/center
hometown: lake charles, louisiana **seasons:** 1962, 1963, 1964

He scored 1,000 career points faster than any player in Kentucky history, reaching the select figure in the 19th game of his second varsity season. By the time Nash finished up at UK, he had scored 1,770 points, a figure that now stands eighth on the Wildcats' all-time list. The 6-5 forward/center led Kentucky in scoring and rebounding in all three of his seasons—and the numbers were impressive. He compiled scoring averages of 23.4, 20.6 and 24 points and rebound marks of 13.2, 12 and 11.7. Had he been blessed with a stronger supporting cast, Nash might have carried UK to postseason greatness. As it was, Kentucky won just one NCAA Tournament game during his career. That came in Nash's sophomore season, 1961-62, when he helped Kentucky to a 23-3 record. Nash scored 30 or more points nine times that season, and he had 23 in the Cats' victory over Butler in the Mideast Regional. But he made just 5 of 19 field-goal attempts and finished with 14 points in a loss to Ohio State and Jerry Lucas (33 points) in the Mideast final. Nash was solid in 1962-63, but Kentucky slid to 16-9 and out of postseason contention. The Wildcats were far better in Nash's final year (his consensus All-American season), boasting a 21-6 record and making the NCAA tourney. The Louisianan went on to play two seasons of pro basketball and briefly was a major league baseball player.

Cats to Remember

cawood ledford

broadcaster, 1954-1992

For many UK fans, Cawood Ledford was their link to Kentucky basketball. He never made a basket or grabbed a rebound, but his deep, mellifluous voice brought the team to the hills and hollows of the state. Many a future Wildcats player first dreamed of playing for the university while listening to Ledford as a young fan.

The Kentucky native began as the "voice of the Wildcats" in 1953-54, moving to Lexington from Harlan to take over for Claude Sullivan, no slouch at the microphone himself. It was a job Ledford would hold for 39 seasons, first as an employee of affiliates throughout the state and later as play-by-play man for the program's statewide network. During his tenure, Ledford called some of the program's greatest moments and became as important to Kentucky basketball as just about anyone else.

Even though Memorial Coliseum and later Rupp Arena were among the largest venues of their times, most UK fans couldn't find room in either jam-packed facility, were stuck on ticket waiting lists, just couldn't make the long trip to Lexington, or couldn't afford to attend games. So, they turned to Ledford. They listened on tiny affiliates in the eastern part of the state, sometimes perching their cars on hills in an attempt to get better reception. Out west, the fans sometimes drove miles to get the signal. If Kentucky basketball had a mythical quality, then Ledford was its Aesop, spinning basketball tales to a rapt audience.

So renowned and popular was Ledford that when Rick Pitino took over at Kentucky in 1989-90, he made it a point to connect with the popular announcer. The on-court Pitino/Ledford postgame show was extremely successful, and Rupp Arena crowds stuck around in great numbers to listen.

Ledford didn't just handle basketball play-by-play. He called football and baseball games and developed a reputation as one of the nation's best horse-racing announcers. Ledford was named Kentucky Broadcaster of the Year 22 times and was elected to the Kentucky athletic and journalism Halls of Fame. He also had his "jersey" retired by the university.

After Ledford called his last game in March 1992—it was the memorable NCAA East Regional final in which Duke defeated Kentucky in overtime on Christian Laettner's buzzer-beating shot—the great tradition of UK basketball continued, only the accompanying soundtrack wasn't quite the same.

derek anderson

1996·1997

Anderson appeared destined to be one of the truly special Wildcats, but a knee injury in his senior season ended his career prematurely. The 6-5 Anderson, who transferred to UK after two years at Ohio State, was a solid contributor on Kentucky's 1996 NCAA championship team, averaging 9.4 points. He scored 11 points in the title game against Syracuse. Anderson was averaging 17.7 points in 1996-97 when he went down in the 18th game of the season. Despite the knee injury that limited him to only a token appearance (to shoot two free throws in the Final Four win over Minnesota) in the spring, he nonetheless was the 13th overall selection (Cleveland) in the 1997 NBA draft.

dwight anderson

1979

Anderson exploded on the scene and then disappeared just as quickly. But while at UK, he gave the Cats a swift, athletic backcourt scorer. As a freshman in 1978-79, Anderson averaged 13.3 points. His 17 second-half points sparked a comeback win over Notre Dame and showcased his skills. Later that season, he scored 26 points against Mississippi State and 25 vs. Florida. A wrist fracture sustained in the 1979 SEC Tournament ended his season. He returned to UK in the fall of '79, and big things were expected of him. But in late December, Anderson left Lexington for "personal reasons." He wound up transferring to Southern California.

jim andrews

1971·1972·1973

Although his name isn't often mentioned when fans debate the great Kentucky centers of all time, Andrews was highly productive for UK. The 6-11 Ohioan played two years for Adolph Rupp and one season under Joe B. Hall and was an All-SEC player for both coaches. As a junior, Andrews averaged 21.5 points and 11.3 rebounds. His biggest outburst that season was a 34-point, 19-board effort against Mississippi State. Andrews was just as effective the next season, 1972-73, finishing with 20.1 and 12.4 scoring and rebounding averages.

cliff barker

1947·1948·1949

Whenever UK's Fabulous Five is revisited, Barker's name usually comes up fourth or fifth. But his ballhandling and passing skills made him just as important to that team as the big guns. Barker's Kentucky career was interrupted by a lengthy stay in the military, and the 6-2 standout was 27 years old when the Fabulous Five made its NCAA Tournament and Olympic Games runs in 1948. A prisoner in World War II, Barker returned to Lexington and was a reserve on the 1946-47 Kentucky team (34-3 record) before playing prominent roles the next two seasons for UK's NCAA championship teams.

dale barnstable

1947·1948·1949·1950

The 6-3 Barnstable, who was from Illinois, was a member of two NCAA championship teams and played on other Kentucky teams that finished 34-3 and 25-5. Barnstable was the No. 5 scorer on the 1948-49 national titlists, averaging 6.1 points, and he was named to the All-Southeastern Conference third team that season. Also the fifth-leading UK scorer (5.9) in 1949-50, he went on an 18-point spree against Vanderbilt as his college career wound down.

ed beck
1956·1957·1958

Beck didn't light up the scoreboard too often, but he was a two-time UK captain and a senior member of the Wildcats' 1958 national championship team. The 6-7 Beck enjoyed his finest statistical season in 1956-57, when he averaged 9.5 points and 14.1 rebounds (the fifth-highest board average in school history). Although his numbers fell the following year, he was an interior stalwart on the Kentucky squad that stumbled to six losses in the regular season but regrouped to win it all.

winston bennett
1984·1985·1986·1988

A chiseled strongman from Louisville, the 6-7 Bennett finished his Kentucky career with 1,399 points. Although he missed the 1986-87 season because of a knee injury, he still played four years at UK. Bennett was at his best as a senior in 1987-88, averaging 15.3 points and a team-leading 7.8 rebounds. It was a season in which Bennett posted career highs in points (28, against Miami of Ohio) and rebounds (17, against Vanderbilt). His scoring averages climbed each season at Kentucky. He later spent three years as a member of Rick Pitino's UK coaching staff.

jerry bird
1954·1955·1956

Bird got into four games as a member of the undefeated 1953-54 Wildcats but was known more for his play the following two seasons—and for the fact that three brothers played football at Kentucky. A 6-6 forward, Bird averaged 10.7 points as a junior and 16.2 points as senior. He scored 34 points against Dayton in December 1955 in the UK Invitational title game. Bird, who was from Corbin in the eastern Kentucky hills, was a strong inside player. Although the Wildcats lost to Iowa in a 1956 NCAA Tournament regional final, Bird scored 23 points against the Hawkeyes.

keith bogans

2000·2001·2002

Powerful and relentless, Bogans came to
Kentucky in the fall of 1999 as a McDonald's
All-American from fabled DeMatha High
School in suburban Washington, D.C. The
guard made an immediate mark with his
ability to score and willingness to play
physical defense. A strong driver and capable
finisher near the basket, he averaged 12.5
points as a freshman and 17 as a sophomore.
Although falling off to an 11.6 mark as a
junior in 2001-02, Bogans closed the season
with scoring outputs of 21, 19 and 15 points
against Valparaiso, Tulsa and Maryland in the
NCAA Tournament.

sam bowie
1980·1981·1984

The 7-1 Bowie arrived from Lebanon, Pa.,
as a heralded recruit. He left as something
of a disappointment after a stress fracture
robbed him of two seasons. Bowie stood
out as a freshman, his averages of 12.9
points, 8.1 rebounds and 2.1 blocks
helping the 1979-80 Cats to 29 victories.
As a sophomore, Bowie led Kentucky in
scoring (17.4 average) and rebounding
(9.1). But he missed the next two seasons
before returning in 1983-84 to help
Kentucky to the Final Four with 10.5 and
9.2 scoring and rebounding figures. In a
what-might-have-been performance, he had
a 20-point, 19-rebound outing against Ole
Miss late in his final season.

bob brannum

1944·1947

The 1943-44 Wildcats were so young that some wag called them the "Wildkittens." But UK had Bob Brannum, and that was enough to secure an SEC Tournament title and advancement to the NIT semifinals. The 6-5 freshman from Kansas (Adolph Rupp's home state) led the team with a 12.1 scoring average. He earned consensus All-American honors and helped Kentucky to big wins over Notre Dame and Cincinnati with 14- and 18-point performances. Brannum transferred to Michigan State after the season but returned in the fall of 1946. He was a mere reserve on the talent-laden '46-'47 Wildcats.

bob burrow

1955·1956

Another notable Kentucky pivot, Burrow was a junior college legend in Texas before coming to Lexington. He was a two-year stalwart at Kentucky and still shares the school mark for rebounds in one game—34. His 17.7 rebound average in 1954-55 remains a UK record. Burrow also is one of just three Wildcats to score 50 or more points in a game. He hit exactly 50 against LSU on January 14, 1956, making 19 of 26 field-goal attempts and 12 of 15 free-throw tries. In a monster performance, he also collected 23 rebounds in that game.

gerry calvert

1955·1956·1957

Calvert scored only 59 points in his first varsity season—but 19 of them came in a 1955 NCAA Tournament game against Penn State, which signaled good times were ahead. The aggressive guard was a key member of the next two Kentucky teams, averaging 11.2 points in 1955-56 and 15.2 in 1956-57. Calvert signed with Louisville after playing high school ball in Maysville, but he changed his mind when Kentucky offered a scholarship. It was a good decision for both sides, with Calvert realizing a childhood dream and UK earning the services of a steady backcourt operative and future captain.

burgess carey

1925·1926

Don't look for Carey's name among the great Kentucky scorers. In fact, it wasn't shocking when the 6-footer went scoreless. He is, however, on the roll of great UK players, thanks to his defensive skill. Carey played two seasons at Kentucky as a "back guard," and he used his rugged frame to keep opponents away from the hoop. He played his role well enough to win All-American recognition in 1924-25. The next season, Carey's stellar defense helped UK win 15 of 18 games. And Carey, a Lexington product, even broke loose for five points in one game.

mike casey

1968·1969·1971

It took exactly one game for Casey to showcase his talents—in his UK debut on December 2, 1967, he scored 28 points at Michigan. Casey came to Lexington as part of a terrific class that included Dan Issel and Mike Pratt. A 6-4 guard with an accurate shooting eye and the ability to step up in crucial situations, Casey led the Wildcats in scoring as a sophomore with a 20-point average. He scored 19.1 points per game the following season but was sidelined in 1969-70 because of a leg fracture suffered in a car accident. Casey returned for one more season and averaged 17 points, although he wasn't as quick as he had been.

rex chapman

1987·1988

Few players generated as much interest during their time at Kentucky as Chapman did. "King Rex" had tremendous range on his jump shot and was able to dunk over much taller opponents. A prep All-American from Owensboro, the 6-5 Chapman was an immediate sensation, scoring 18 points in his debut against Austin Peay and smoking Louisville for 26 a month later. He set a UK freshman record with 464 points. Chapman opted for the NBA draft after two seasons at Kentucky. In his UK finale, he scored 30 points against Villanova in an NCAA Tournament game.

truman claytor

1976·1977·1978·1979

Claytor was a solid backcourt contributor who played behind and with Kyle Macy on the strong UK teams of the late 1970s. Claytor is perhaps best remembered for his strong play early in the 1978 NCAA Tournament—he scored a team-high 16 points against Florida State and made six of seven field-goal attempts against Miami of Ohio. In the '78 NCAA title game, he scored eight points as the Cats defeated Duke. He averaged a career-high 8.7 points in 1978-79, his senior season.

bennie coffman

1959·1960

Junior college transfer Coffman, a guard who played his high school ball in West Virginia, came aboard the season after the Wildcats won the NCAA title in 1958. UK's backcourt needed shoring up after Vernon Hatton and Adrian Smith completed their careers as key members of the '58 champions. Coffman averaged 10.7 points in 1958-59—the third-best figure on a Kentucky team that went 24-3—and scored at a 10.2 clip the next season. As a senior, he sank 88.2 percent of his free-throw attempts.

sid cohen

1959·1960

The 6-1 Cohen, a junior college transfer, spent two seasons at UK and played largely in supporting roles. He was a member of a backcourt rotation in 1958-59 that included Dicky Parsons, Billy Ray Lickert and Bennie Coffman. Cohen, who was from Brooklyn, averaged 8.1 points as Kentucky won 24 of 27 games. As a senior, Cohen boosted his scoring average to 10.7—the third-best figure for the 1959-60 Wildcats, who finished 18-7.

larry conley

1964·1965·1966

Adolph Rupp called Conley "a coach on the floor." Perhaps the most accurate passer in Kentucky history, Conley was a tough-as-nails 6-3 forward—despite a slender frame. He averaged 12.2 points as a sophomore on UK's 1963-64 team and scored 11.6 points per game the following season. But it was Conley's sharp passing and unselfish play during his senior season—he also averaged 11.5 points—that helped make Rupp's Runts so dangerous and, ultimately, the 1966 national runner-up. Conley led the Wildcats in assists in all three of his varsity seasons.

jimmy dan conner

1973·1974·1975

A Kentucky high school hero, Conner made his UK debut in 1972-73 as a member of Joe B. Hall's first Wildcats team and established himself as a steady swingman. He averaged 11.2 points and a team-leading three assists. A strong defender, Conner scored 12 points per game as a junior on a disappointing 13-13 club. But he was a key cog on the Wildcats' 1975 national runner-up team, finishing second to Kevin Grevey in scoring with a 12.4 mark. He scored 35 points against North Carolina early in the season and came up big (17 points) in the Cats' Mideast Regional final upset of previously unbeaten Indiana.

fred cowan
1978·1979·1980·1981

In an era dominated by the likes of Jack Givens, Kyle Macy and Sam Bowie, it's easy to lose track of Cowan. But the 6-8 frontcourt player lettered four times and was a major presence around the basket. He was a deep reserve on UK's 1978 national championship team but saw steady duty the next three seasons. Cowan's highest scoring average was 12.5 points, in 1979-80. He was at his best when he scored 26 points—nearly half of Kentucky's total—and pulled down six rebounds in a 55-54 loss to Duke in the 1980 Mideast Regional semifinals.

johnny cox
1957·1958·1959

There were dozens of highlights during Cox's three varsity seasons with the Wildcats, but he is probably best remembered for his 24-point outburst in Kentucky's triumph over Seattle in the 1958 NCAA championship game. The 6-4 junior clinched the crown for the Cats by scoring 16 points in the game's final 15 minutes. A roughneck from the hills of eastern Kentucky, Cox averaged 17.4 points and 12 rebounds in his UK career. As a senior, a year in which he won consensus All-American honors, he put on a dazzling 38-point, 17-rebound show against Tennessee.

john crigler

1956·1957·1958

The UK coaching staff considered Crigler an unsung star on the 1958 Fiddlin' Five, and that designation was certainly true in that year's national title win over Seattle. Sure, Crigler scored 14 points, but the forward's biggest contribution was luring Seattle star Elgin Baylor into foul trouble. Crigler was a two-year starter at Kentucky, averaging 10.3 points in 1956-57 and 13.6 (third-best on the team) for Kentucky's NCAA champions. His 26 points and 16 rebounds against Ole Miss on February 8, 1958, attracted plenty of attention—but his effort six weeks later against Baylor and company attracted even more.

ed davender

1985·1986·1987·1988

Davender's name doesn't roll off the tongues of Kentucky fans when they discuss UK's foremost players, but there is no denying the guard's significant contributions to the program. He's the only player in school history to score 1,500 points (he finished with 1,637) and record 400 assists (he had 436). Davender, who was from Brooklyn, averaged 15.7 points in his senior season of 1987-88. He played on Joe B. Hall's final Kentucky team and was a member of three Eddie Sutton-coached squads. In the 1988 NCAA Tournament, he scored 30 points against Southern and 23 against Maryland.

ted deeken

1962·1963·1964

A product of the Louisville prep ranks, Deeken became a regular at Kentucky midway through his junior year and averaged 9.8 points that season (1962-63). He had a breakout performance as a senior, pouring in 18.5 points per game. The 6-3 forward teamed with Cotton Nash to give the Wildcats a strong interior, and at times he surpassed his more celebrated frontcourt partner. Deeken scored 20 or more points 10 times during the 1963-64 season, notching 34 against Auburn (Nash had 33 in that game) and 29 against both Northwestern and Georgia.

john de moisey

1932·1933·1934

"Frenchy" was a 6-4 center who, under Adolph Rupp's tutelage, perfected a hook shot. He twice was an All-Southeastern Conference selection and won All-American honors as a senior in 1933-34, a season in which he averaged 12.3 points and the Cats finished 16-1. DeMoisey went on a 25-point spree against Vanderbilt in the next-to-last game of his UK career. As a junior, DeMoisey teamed with Forest Sale to lead the Wildcats to the championship of the first SEC Tournament.

leroy edwards

1935

It may be hard to think of the 6-4 Edwards as a giant, but that was a fitting description for him. Edwards, who played only one season at UK before entering pro ball, was so strong that opposing teams often resorted to extremely physical play in an attempt to control him—usually to no avail. Edwards alone outscored the Wildcats' first five opponents in 1934-35, and he averaged 16.3 points over Kentucky's 21-game schedule. His 34 points against Creighton set a school record. Edwards was a consensus All-American in '34-'35 and the Helms Athletic Foundation's national Player of the Year.

billy evans

1952·1954·1955

Twice UK's leading free-throw shooter, Evans was a member of the undefeated 1953-54 Wildcats. He averaged 8.4 points that season, the fourth-best mark on the team. The 6-1 Evans scored 13.9 points per game in 1954-55, his final season, and he got 20 against defending NCAA champion La Salle in Kentucky's 63-54 victory in the championship game of the UK Invitational. The forward/guard was ruled ineligible for the 1955 NCAA Tournament because of his fifth-year status. Evans played on the 1956 U.S. Olympic team that won a gold medal in Melbourne.

richie farmer

1989·1990·1991·1992

A Clay County High School sensation, he ranks as perhaps the most popular prep player in Kentucky history. Not a physically gifted player, Farmer posted a career scoring average of only 7.6 points at UK, but the guard's dedication to the program was second to none. He won lasting fame as a member of Rick Pitino's 1991-92 Unforgettables, players who were recruited by another staff but persevered through the probation handed down during that earlier regime and nearly made the Final Four as seniors. Farmer had a 28-point game against Notre Dame in that memorable '91-'92 season.

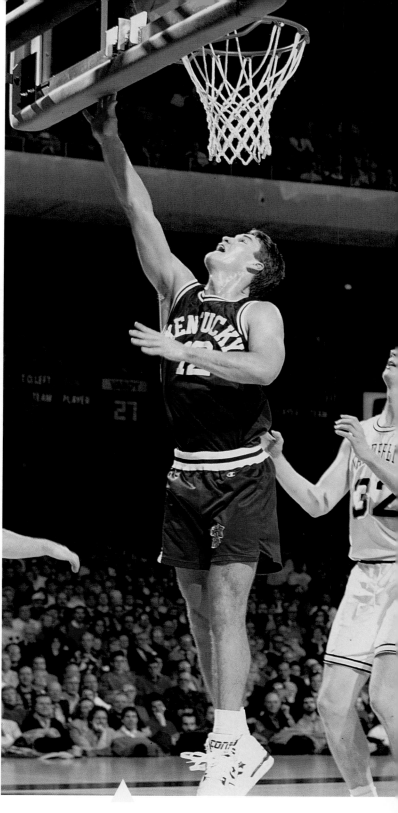

deron feldhaus

1989·1990·1991·1992

Possessing a UK pedigree, Feldhaus was a key player on Rick Pitino's Unforgettables and a member of Kentucky's 1,000-point club. The son of early-1960s Wildcat Allen Feldhaus, Deron played for his father at Mason County High School. Feldhaus, a 6-7 forward, was a double-figure scorer for UK in his final three seasons, managing a career-high 14.4 points per game as a sophomore in 1989-90. He gave the Wildcats a rare blend of interior toughness and perimeter shooting accuracy.

travis ford

1992·1993·1994

A prep standout at Madisonville North Hopkins, Ford came "home" to UK in 1990 after spending his freshman year at Missouri. He backed up Sean Woods during his first season (1991-92) with the Wildcats and then became the starting point guard for his final two years. Displaying a sweet outside stroke and a deadly eye from the foul line, Ford set a UK season record with 101 3-point field goals in 1992-93 and wound up as the Wildcats' No. 2 career free-throw shooter (88.2 percent accuracy). He scored 13.6 points per game in '92-'93. A smooth distributor, he averaged 5.8 assists as a senior in '93-'94.

phil grawemeyer

1954·1955·1956

The 6-7 forward was a stalwart on the 1954-55 Wildcats, averaging 13 points, but a leg fracture suffered in a February game against DePaul ended his season and perhaps cost Kentucky a chance to advance beyond the regional semifinals of the NCAA Tournament. In December 1954, he had a 28-point game against LSU and a 27-point outing against Utah. Grawemeyer returned for his senior season in 1955-56, earning his third letter at UK, but his production dropped to 8.4 points per game.

reggie hanson

1988·1989·1990·1991

Hanson had a slow start at UK, but the 6-7 forward/center blossomed as a junior member of Rick Pitino's first team in Lexington. He averaged 16.4 points and 7.1 rebounds for that 1989-90 squad that finished with a 14-14 record. His production the following season—14.4 points and 7.2 rebounds per game—helped Kentucky to a surprising 22-6 record. Hanson's quickness and athletic ability gave the Wildcats a substantial interior presence during years in which Kentucky began to reassert itself after reaching the depths in 1988-89 with a 13-19 mark.

vernon hatton

1956·1957·1958

Folks still talk about Hatton's performance in the 1958 Final Four against Temple and Seattle. Hatton, a 6-3 senior guard, had excelled earlier that season in a win over Temple, sinking a 47-foot heave to force a second overtime and then scoring UK's last six points in the third extra session. Then, in the teams' meeting in the national semifinals, Hatton made a layup with 16 seconds remaining that gave Kentucky a 61-60 victory over the Owls. Hatton followed up with a 30-point spree against Seattle in the NCAA title game, which the Wildcats won, 84-72. In his three varsity seasons, he averaged 13.3, 14.8 and 17.1 points.

basil hayden

1920·1921·1922

Kentucky has a long list of All-Americans, but Hayden was the first. The guard/forward from Paris, Ky., averaged 10.8 points as a sophomore in 1919-20 and scored 9.6 points per game in 1920-21, a season in which he won All-American honors and helped the Wildcats to a 13-1 record. A knee injury limited his production as a senior—he averaged only five points per game as the Cats fell off to a 10-6 mark—but Hayden's place in UK lore is secure.

walt hirsch

1949·1950·1951

A 6-4 forward, Hirsch was a member of the 1948-49 and 1950-51 Kentucky teams that won national championships (although he was ruled ineligible for the 1951 NCAA Tournament because he was a fourth-year varsity player). Hirsch averaged 4.6 points as a top reserve for the '49 titlists and was a 9.1 scorer for the '51 kingpins. In 1949-50, he was the No. 3 scorer (9.9 average) behind Bill Spivey and Jim Line as the Wildcats compiled a 25-5 record. Hirsch was from Dayton, Ohio.

derrick hord

1980·1981·1982·1983

When Hord signed with the Wildcats in 1979, he was expected to be the next great Kentucky player. Although the 6-6 swingman from Tennessee did finish with 1,220 career points, he had just one standout season, 1981-82, when he averaged a team-best 16.3 points and earned All-SEC honors. The sleek wing was outstanding at times that year, scoring 28 points against Akron, 26 vs. Vanderbilt and 24 against LSU. He couldn't duplicate his great junior year in 1982-83, though, his scoring average dropping to 8.9.

lee huber
1939·1940·1941

Huber was supposed to be hitting the ball over the net, not putting it into the net. Arriving at Kentucky on a tennis scholarship in the late 1930s after twice winning the state prep title, Huber soon became a key member of the Wildcats' basketball team. In 1939-40, the 6-foot guard from Louisville scored 17 points against Clemson and had three other double-figure efforts. Possessor of a dazzling set shot, Huber had seven double-digit scoring outbursts in 1940-41.

thad jaracz
1966·1967·1968

Although Jaracz was overshadowed by more celebrated players during his UK career, he nonetheless distinguished himself as a three-time double-figure scorer and as a key member of Rupp's Runts, the 1966 national runner-up. Despite standing just 6-5, Jaracz played center for the Runts—he was their lone sophomore starter—and averaged 13.2 points. He scored 11.3 points per game each of the next two seasons and led Kentucky in rebounding (8.3 average) as a junior. As a senior in 1967-68, he scored 25 points and pulled down 18 rebounds in a victory over Georgia. Jaracz finished his career with 982 points.

ellis johnson
1931·1932·1933

Johnson's smart playmaking and stout defense made him a three-year letterman and even earned him All-American honors in 1933. Johnson also was an accomplished football player (three UK letters) and spent time on Kentucky's baseball and track teams. Johnson came to UK the year before Adolph Rupp took over the basketball team, and he earned a starting berth on the Baron's first team, the 1930-31 squad. The 6-foot guard left the scoring to the likes of Carey Spicer, Forest "Aggie" Sale and John DeMoisey, but Johnson had his moments—including a 14-point game against Tennessee-Chattanooga when he was a junior.

tommy kron
1964·1965·1966

Adolph Rupp probably wouldn't have stayed with the 1-3-1 zone during the 1965-66 season had it not been for Kron's aggressive play at the point of the defense. Though sharing the distinction as the tallest member of the starting lineup at 6-5, Kron played in the backcourt for Rupp's Runts. A steady offensive player, he scored 10.2 points per game as a senior in '65-'66 and helped the Runts reach the NCAA championship game. Kron had 14 points and nine rebounds in UK's Mideast Regional final victory over Michigan, and he got 12 points and 10 rebounds in the national semifinals against Duke. He averaged 12.3 points in 1964-65.

dave lawrence
1933·1934·1935

Lawrence wasn't one of the biggest names at Kentucky during the mid-1930s, but All-American selectors certainly were aware of him. A part-time starter as a sophomore, Lawrence was a regular as a junior in 1933-34 and averaged 7.9 points. As a senior co-captain, the forward scored 9.1 points per game, helped propel the Wildcats to a 19-2 record and won All-American honors (as did teammate Leroy Edwards). Lawrence hit double-figure point totals nine times in 1934-35, with a 23-point outburst against Tennessee-Chattanooga his best effort.

james lee

1975·1976·1977·1978

Playing alongside stars like Jack Givens, Kyle Macy and Rick Robey, a player needed something special to be noticed. For Lee, a 6-5 forward, it was power dunking (which he exhibited most memorably at the conclusion of the 1978 NCAA title game, right). A bruising presence inside yet athletic enough to be a valuable weapon in the open court, Lee was a key role player on the '78 NCAA championship team. He averaged 11.3 points that season and had 13 points and eight rebounds against Arkansas in the national semifinals. Lee became a starter as a sophomore, on the 1975-76 NIT title team, when Robey suffered an injury. Lee just missed membership in UK's 1,000-point club, finishing his career with 996 points.

billy ray lickert

1959·1960·1961

Lickert's career statistics aren't awe-inspiring—1,076 career points, 14.7 scoring average—but he was capable of some tremendous single-game performances. Among the finest for this 6-3 Kentucky swingman were his 24-point, 17-rebound effort against Notre Dame on February 14, 1959; a stretch in 1960-61 when, in four consecutive games, he got 29 points against Saint Louis, 29 against Missouri, 23 against Miami of Ohio and 25 against Georgia Tech; and a 28-point outing against Morehead State in the 1961 NCAA Tournament. Lickert was an All-SEC selection in '61.

jim line

1947·1948·1949·1950

Line never achieved "fabulous" status as a sophomore on Kentucky's 1948 national champions, but the 6-2 forward from Akron, Ohio, did average seven points, the fourth-best figure on the team. As a starter for UK's 1949 NCAA titlists, he scored only 5.7 points per game but came up big in the NCAA Tournament with a 21-point effort against Villanova and a 15-point performance against Illinois. As a senior in 1949-50, Line was Kentucky's No. 2 scorer with a 13.1 average. In Line's four seasons on the UK varsity—he also saw extensive duty as a freshman—the Wildcats compiled a 127-13 record.

shelby linville

1950·1951·1952

Although Kentucky's 1951 national championship team was led by 7-foot center Bill Spivey, Linville was a strong second-in-command. The 6-5 junior forward averaged 10.4 points that season and had some big games. Most notable was his 23-point, 10-rebound outing against Louisville in the NCAA Tournament. In 1951-52, Linville had All-American potential but found it difficult to get adequate playing time. Adolph Rupp was reluctant to play him full time, apparently thinking Linville might have been involved in some way in the gambling scandal that had jolted the program. He wasn't involved, and Rupp later apologized.

jamaal magloire

1997·1998·1999·2000

The 6-10 center from Canada is Kentucky's career blocked-shots leader with 268 rejections. He had three blocks and seven points in the 1998 NCAA championship game against Utah. Magloire, who scored 1,064 points as a Wildcat and pulled down 789 rebounds, was named UK's best defender in his last three seasons and tied Wayne Turner for the honor as a freshman. He averaged a career-best 13.2 points in his senior season of 1999-00.

jim master
1981·1982·1983·1984

Had there been a 3-point rule during Master's career, the 6-5 shooter would have finished with considerably more than 1,283 points. Master became a starter during his sophomore season, 1981-82, and he wound up as UK's No. 2 scorer with a 13.4 average. His numbers then slipped, to 12.5 as a junior and 9.6 as a senior, as the cast around him improved. But Master was always a contributor—thanks to his zone-busting shooting skill and free-throw accuracy (84.9 percent over four seasons). In the 1984 NCAA Tournament, he scored 13 points against Brigham Young and 15 vs. Louisville.

paul mcbrayer
1928·1929·1930

He was a starter in the three seasons immediately preceding Adolph Rupp's arrival. The 6-4 guard earned All-American recognition in 1929-30 despite scoring just 4.8 points per game (although UK's leading scorer, Cecil Combs, finished at only 6.6). McBrayer was a heady player and team captain who helped Kentucky to a 40-14 record during his years as a regular. He became Rupp's first long-term assistant, serving under the Baron for nine years beginning with the 1934-35 season. He made significant contributions with his recruiting and tactical abilities.

walter mccarty
1994·1995·1996

An active frontcourt player, he was a key member of the Wildcats' 1996 national championship team. The 6-10 McCarty was an exciting player, fast for his size and an amazing leaper. He averaged 5.7 points as a sophomore reserve on the 1993-94 team and became a starter the following year. McCarty scored 10.5 points per game as a junior and had 17 points and 11 rebounds in UK's first-round NCAA Tournament victory over Mount St. Mary's. His senior season was the best—in addition to scoring at an 11.3 clip, McCarty led the Wildcats with 1.4 blocks per game and a .543 field-goal percentage.

ron mercer
1996·1997

A Tennessean who was the subject of a heated recruiting battle between his home-state Volunteers and Kentucky, the 6-7 Mercer was practically impossible to stop on his way to the hoop but also could fill it up from the outside. As a freshman, he scored 20 points in Kentucky's victory over Syracuse in the 1996 NCAA title game. He blossomed as a sophomore, averaging 18.1 points and winning SEC Player of the Year and consensus All-American honors. He turned pro after two seasons at UK and was the sixth overall pick (Boston) in the 1997 NBA draft.

derrick miller
1987·1988·1989·1990

If there was a player made for Rick Pitino's run-and-gun system, it was Miller. He averaged 19.2 points as a senior on Pitino's first Kentucky team, quite a reversal of fortunes for someone who considered leaving UK after seeing sparse playing time as a sophomore. The 6-5 guard had tremendous shooting range—he stands second on the Wildcats' career list with 191 3-pointers. Miller converted 35.8 percent of his long-range shots over four seasons. He set a school record for most points scored at Rupp Arena, sinking six treys on the way to a 40-point spree against Vanderbilt on February 7, 1990.

don mills

1958·1959·1960

Mills was a reserve on Kentucky's 1958 national champions, but his nine points and five rebounds in the title game against Seattle were huge. His hook shot in the second half pushed Kentucky ahead, 61-60—the Wildcats had trailed the Chieftains by 11 points at one juncture—and the Cats went on to win, 84-72. The 6-6 center/forward was a solid interior presence for three years in Lexington. He started two of those seasons, averaging 10.5 points in 1958-59 and 12.7 (the second-best figure on the team) in 1959-60. He pulled down 12.9 rebounds per game as a senior.

dirk minniefield

1980·1981·1982·1983

Minniefield was an old-school point guard who lived to set up his teammates. The 6-3 Lexington product was so good in the early 1980s that he remains Kentucky's all-time leader in assists (646). His 6.3 assists average in 1981-82, his junior season, is the second-best figure in school history. Minniefield also led the Cats in steals three consecutive years. But Minniefield wasn't just a passer and defender. He twice posted double-figure scoring averages and finished with 1,069 points. As a junior, he had a 25-point game against Alabama.

nazr mohammed

1996·1997·1998

Mohammed left Kentucky after only one productive year—his junior season of 1997-98, in which he scored 12 points per game for UK's national champions and posted team-high averages of 7.2 rebounds and 1.9 blocked shots. He scored 18 points against Stanford in the '98 national semifinals, then got 10 points against Utah in the title game. He also was a member of UK's 1996 NCAA titlists, although he played sparingly that season. As a sophomore on Rick Pitino's last team, which lost to Arizona in the 1997 national championship game, the 6-10 Mohammed averaged 7.9 points and 5.8 rebounds.

bernard opper

1937·1938·1939

Give Opper credit for ingenuity. The New Yorker liked what he saw when Kentucky played at Madison Square Garden, so he wrote Adolph Rupp a letter asking for a chance to play for the Wildcats. He made the most of his opportunity, becoming a reliable ballhandler, passer and defender for three seasons beginning in 1936-37. Although he never averaged more than 5.6 points (1937-38), Opper helped UK to two SEC Tournament titles and won All-American recognition in 1939. The guard scored 13 points in the Cats' win over Tennessee in the '39 SEC tourney final.

scott padgett

1995·1997·1998·1999

Padgett spent 18 months away from UK basketball because of a cavalier attitude toward classwork. The Louisville product saw limited time for the Wildcats in 1994-95 as a freshman before leaving school to work back home. The 6-9 forward returned with a vengeance and became one of the program's most revered clutch scorers. Padgett averaged 11.5 points in 1997-98 and 12.6 in 1998-99. He scored a Kentucky-high 17 points in both the 1997 NCAA championship game loss to Arizona and the 1998 NCAA final victory over Utah. He became a two-time All-SEC academic choice and twice was named to All-Final Four teams.

tom parker

1970·1971·1972

In his third varsity appearance, sophomore Parker came off the bench in December 1969 and scored 15 points against Indiana. A great shooter, the 6-7 forward from Collinsville, Ill., cracked the starting lineup in the second half of that season and scored in double figures in UK's last 11 games. Parker then led the Wildcats with a 17.6 scoring average in 1970-71 and had 23 points in the Cats' NCAA Tournament loss to Western Kentucky. He improved his output to 18 points per game as a senior and scored 30 against Notre Dame. Parker finished his UK career with 1,238 points.

jack parkinson

1944·1945·1946·1948

Parkinson had two UK careers. His first—and more productive—came in the three seasons before he served in the military. The 6-foot guard was a starter on the 1943-44 team that finished third in the NIT. A freshman that season, he scored seven points per game. Parkinson averaged 10.4 points as a sophomore, then won All-American honors in 1945-46 when he led the NIT champion Wildcats with an 11.3 scoring mark. He had double-figure point totals in eight consecutive games in February/March of '46. After a stint in the service, Parkinson played a bit role for Kentucky's 1947-48 national champions.

tom payne

1971

Payne holds a special place in Kentucky history as Adolph Rupp's first black recruit. But rather than serving as a strong force after shattering the color barrier, Payne withered under the racial epithets that were hurled his way on the road. Athletic but extremely raw, the 7-2 Payne had a solid sophomore season in 1970-71. He was particularly devastating in consecutive games against Georgia (34 points, 15 rebounds) and LSU (39 points, 19 rebounds). Overall, he averaged 16.9 points and 10.1 rebounds. But that was it. Payne declared himself a hardship case after the season and turned pro with the NBA's Atlanta Hawks.

john pelphrey

1989·1990·1991·1992

A three-time all-state player at Paintsville High School, Pelphrey arrived at UK less-equipped athletically than many of his future teammates and opponents, but his work ethic made him a substantial contributor to the UK program. Pelphrey became a starter as a sophomore in 1989-90, scoring 13 points per game for Rick Pitino's first Wildcats team. The forward shared the team lead in scoring as a junior with a 14.4 mark and averaged 12.5 points in 1991-92. One of UK's Unforgettables, he stepped up his game in the '92 NCAA Tournament and scored 22, 20, 18 and 16 points in the Cats' four games.

mike phillips

1975·1976·1977·1978

It's practically impossible to think of Phillips and not think of Rick Robey. The 6-10 Kentucky players were teammates for four seasons, and they helped the Wildcats win 102 games, one NCAA championship (1978) and an NIT crown (1976). Phillips and Robey also were members of an NCAA Tournament runner-up team (1975). Though Phillips is forever linked with his fellow frontcourt operative, he had a solid identity of his own. He finished with 1,367 points at UK, led the Cats in rebounding in 1975-76 (9.8 per game) and made 54.9 percent of his career field-goal attempts. Phillips averaged a career-high 15.6 points as a sophomore.

mike pratt
1968·1969·1970

Pratt finished his Kentucky career with 1,359 points, but he was a supporting actor to Dan Issel's lead. Pratt was equally at home inside and on the perimeter, and the 6-4 forward had few equals at setting picks. The Dayton, Ohio, sharpshooter spent three years as a starter, improving his scoring average from 14.1 to 16.9 to 19.3 (Issel's figures those seasons were 16.4, 26.6 and 33.9). On December 27, 1969, at Freedom Hall in Louisville, Pratt ended up with star billing. He scored 42 points to Issel's 35 in UK's 102-100 victory over Notre Dame. Pratt made 16 of 26 floor shots and all 10 of his free-throw attempts in that game. He and Issel were later teammates (above) with the Kentucky Colonels of the American Basketball Association.

tayshaun prince
1999·2000·2001·2002

One of the more far-flung Kentucky recruits, Prince came to Lexington from California. A spindly 6-9 forward with a sweet shooting touch, he saw part-time starting duty as a freshman in 1998-99 before leading the Cats in scoring as a sophomore (13.3 average) and making a big impression in the 2000 NCAA Tournament with a 28-point outburst against St. Bonaventure. Prince averaged 16.9 points in 2000-01, then ended his career with team-leading 17.5 and 6.3 scoring and rebounding averages. He was at his best in his next-to-last UK game, erupting for 41 points against Tulsa in the 2002 NCAA Tournament. Prince scored 1,775 career points, seventh-highest total in school history.

larry pursiful

1960·1961·1962

Pursiful was a 6-1 guard with a great outside shooting touch. As a senior in 1961-62, he was a dangerous perimeter complement to sophomore Cotton Nash's fine inside game. Pursiful was used sparingly as a sophomore but was a key player as a junior, averaging 13.4 points in 1960-61. He was even more effective in his final season, scoring 19.1 points per game (to Nash's 23.4) and winning All-SEC honors as the Wildcats raced to a 23-3 record. Pursiful was particularly effective against Tennessee that year, with 34- and 30-point games against the Volunteers.

rodrick rhodes

1993·1994·1995

One of the most highly regarded recruits in Kentucky history, Rhodes had played at Jersey City prep power St. Anthony's. Though he was a strong performer at UK, he never became a full-fledged star. The Rhodes hype was fueled by his 27-point performance against Georgia Tech in the second game of his freshman season (1992-93), but the 6-7 forward ended the year with a modest 9.1 scoring average and totaled only 30 points in UK's last eight games. Rhodes scored 14.6 points per game as a sophomore, but his average fell off as a junior (to 12.9) and he eventually transferred to Southern California.

pat riley

1965·1966·1967

A 6-4 forward from Schenectady, N.Y., he was the entire package. He ran, jumped and shot well. He hit the backboards with gusto and played sticky defense. And he had an overwhelming desire to win. As a junior, Riley stood out on UK's 1965-66 national runner-up team, leading the Wildcats in scoring (22 points per game) and rebounding (8.9 average) en route to earning All-American honors. In the NCAA Tournament, he poured in 29 points against both Dayton and Michigan and scored 19 in the Final Four against both Duke and Texas Western. Riley injured his back in the next offseason, but the future NBA coach averaged 17.4 points and a team-high 2.6 assists as a senior.

rick robey
1975·1976·1977·1978

One of the finest big men in a program filled with them, the 6-10 Robey scored 1,395 career points and would have had many more if an injury hadn't limited him to 12 games as a sophomore. The strong yet mobile Robey teamed with Mike Phillips and James Lee to form an imposing front wall in the late 1970s. Robey contributed mightily to Kentucky's 1978 national champions, averaging 14.4 points and a team-high 8.2 rebounds. He scored 20 points and had 11 rebounds in the title game against Duke. Robey led UK in rebounding three times, and his .544 field-goal percentage in 1974-75 remains the best-ever figure by a UK freshman.

kenny rollins
1943·1947·1948

Rollins was the senior on-court leader of Kentucky's 1948 NCAA champions. A two-time All-SEC selection, the 6-foot guard never averaged more than 8.4 points in a season but was a fine passer, ballhandler and defender. His defensive prowess was never more evident than in the '48 NCAA tourney, when he hounded Holy Cross guard Bob Cousy, who managed only five points against UK (about 11 below his average). Despite his modest offensive figures, Rollins gained attention with a 16-point performance against St. John's at Madison Square Garden on December 23, 1947.

gayle rose
1952·1954·1955

A three-time letterman, the 6-foot guard from Paris, Ky., was a bit player on the 1951-52 UK team that went 29-3. Idled when Kentucky's 1952-53 season was suspended, Rose cracked the starting lineup as a junior in '53-'54 and averaged 6.7 points for the 25-0 Wildcats. Rose was a regular again as a senior and posted a career-best 7.4 scoring average. He was superb in the Wildcats' 1955 NCAA tournament loss to Marquette, scoring a game-high 20 points.

forest sale

1931·1932·1933

A two-time consensus All-American, "Aggie" was one of Kentucky's best-ever interior players. The 6-4 Sale struggled with injuries during his sophomore season (1930-31) but rebounded in '31-'32 and led the team in scoring with a 13.8 average. Sale broke loose for 21 points against Tulane and for 20 vs. Washington and Lee. As a senior, Sale again scored 13.8 points per game and was named the national Player of the Year by the Helms Athletic Foundation. Also in '32-'33, he led Kentucky to its first-ever 20-victory season and the inaugural SEC Tournament title as well.

jeff sheppard

1994·1995·1996·1998

Despite spending stretches of his career as a reserve and even being redshirted in his fourth year at UK, Sheppard went out in resounding fashion. The 6-3 guard broke loose for 27 points in the Wildcats' 1998 national semifinal victory over Stanford and contributed 16 points in a comeback win over Utah in the NCAA championship game. Plus, he sank the jump shot that gave Kentucky the lead for good against the Utes. He was named the Final Four's Most Outstanding Player. The exciting, athletic Sheppard, who led the '98 champs in scoring with a 13.7 average, concluded his career with 1,091 points.

adrian smith

1957·1958

Smith, a 6-foot guard, served an apprenticeship in the Mississippi junior college ranks before convincing Adolph Rupp that he was big enough to play big-time basketball. He was a key reserve on Kentucky's 1956-57 team that finished 23-5 team. Smith was a starter on the 1957-58 national champion Wildcats, averaging 12.4 points. His four late free throws helped Kentucky overcome Temple in the Final Four semifinals. Earlier in the NCAA tourney, he scored 18 points against Miami of Ohio and 16 vs. Notre Dame. Smith was a member of the 1960 U.S. Olympic team that won the gold medal in Rome.

carey spicer

1929·1930·1931

A tremendous natural athlete, the 6-1 forward was a two-time basketball All-American and a standout quarterback for the Wildcats. He began his basketball career at UK under coach John Mauer and thrived in his pattern-style offense, averaging 5.7 points as a sophomore (his first All-American season) and 6.5 as a junior. When Adolph Rupp arrived in the fall of 1930, Spicer was up to the challenge of playing at a faster pace. He increased his output to a team-high 10.6 points per game, good for a second All-American honor.

larry steele

1969·1970·1971

Steele overcame injuries to become a valuable member of UK teams that went 71-13 from 1968-69 through 1970-71. Steele broke into the starting lineup as a sophomore forward, averaging 8.6 points. His junior year was marred by an ankle injury that hindered him in the second half of the season. Still, Steele managed 8.8 points per game for a team that scored 100 or more points 13 times. Slowed by a hand injury early in '70-'71, the 6-5 Indianan scored 20 or more points in five games and averaged a career-high 13.1 points.

jack tingle
1944·1945·1946·1947

Tingle earned All-SEC honors four consecutive years, seasons in which UK won 103 of 114 games. Tingle never posted eye-popping statistics, but he was the Cats' No. 2 scorer in 1943-44 (8.4 average) and 1944-45 (11.5). As a junior, the 6-3 forward averaged 9.2 points and helped Kentucky win the 1946 NIT championship. In the NIT semifinals, Tingle scored a game-high 16 points against West Virginia. He wound up his career as a 5.5 scorer on a 1946-47 Wildcats team that finished 34-3.

lou tsioropoulos
1951·1952·1954

He came to Lexington from Lynn, Mass., to play football, but he gave up the gridiron for basketball. Not that he didn't maintain his football toughness. Rebounding and defense were the fortes of the brawny Tsioropoulos, who stood 6-5. As a sophomore, he was a reserve on Kentucky's 1951 national champions. He moved into the starting lineup the following year and scored 7.9 points per night and averaged 10.3 rebounds for a UK team that finished 29-3. Tsioropoulos was at his finest in 1953-54—the season after the one-year suspension of the UK program—when he averaged 14.5 points and 9.6 rebounds.

wayne turner
1996·1997·1998·1999

A slashing guard with tremendous penetration skills, Turner was part of 132 Kentucky wins and two national championships. Not a particularly good outside shooter, Turner could take it to the basket past just about anyone. He finished his career with 1,170 points, averaging a career-best 10.5 as a senior in 1998-99. Turner left UK as the school's all-time leader in steals (238), and he twice paced the Wildcats in assists (a 4.4 average in 1997-98 and a 3.9 mark in '98-'99). As a freshman, he averaged 4.5 points for UK's 1996 national champs. Two years later, he scored 9.3 points per game for Kentucky's NCAA titlists.

melvin turpin

1981·1982·1983·1984

The 6-11 Turpin scored 1,509 points, good for 14th on UK's all-time list, and he twice led the Wildcats in rebounding. He is second on Kentucky's career blocked-shots list with 226 rejections. As a senior in 1983-84, he averaged a team-leading 15.2 points and helped the Cats to the Final Four. He collected a UK-high 15.1 points per game as a junior and scored at a 13.1 clip as a sophomore. Turpin and Sam Bowie are often thought of as a longtime UK frontcourt duo, yet the two were teammates for only two seasons because of Bowie's injury problems.

antoine walker

1995·1996

Walker played just two seasons before leaving for the NBA. A 6-8 forward with good shooting range, he could feed the post and set up teammates on the break—skills that made him a perfect fit for Rick Pitino's system. A Chicagoan who came to Lexington as Pitino began to spread UK's recruiting tentacles throughout the nation, Walker was a reserve on the 1994-95 team that lost to North Carolina in the Southeast Regional final. He was MVP of the 1995 SEC Tournament, scoring 21 points in the semifinals against Florida and 23 in the title game against Arkansas. Walker averaged 15.2 points as a sophomore on UK's 1996 national champs.

bobby watson

1950·1951·1952

Adolph Rupp wondered if this slender, 5-10 point man could handle the workload at Kentucky, but the Baron was soon convinced. Watson made an instant splash, starting on UK's 1949-50 SEC title team as a sophomore and averaging 7.5 points. Watson was a key member of the 1951 national champions, tying for second on the team with a 10.4 scoring average and providing strong outside shooting and solid playmaking. Watson scored 13.1 points per game as a senior. Needing three points in his final UK game to join the Wildcats' 1,000-point club, Watson scored four against St. John's in the NCAA tourney.

sean woods

1990·1991·1992

Woods is probably best remembered for his shot with 2.1 seconds left in overtime against Duke in the 1992 East Regional final—a field goal that sent UK ahead, 103-102. But Kentucky's Unforgettables, with a trip to the Final Four seemingly in hand, fell victim to Christian Laettner's ensuing heroics. Woods, a senior, scored 21 points in that game. He led the Wildcats in assists in all three of his UK seasons. He was the starting point man on Rick Pitino's first UK team in 1989-90, averaging 9.1 points and 5.9 assists. He scored 9.7 and 7.7 points per game in 1990-91 and '91-'92.

Arenas

alumni gym

Talk about your home-court advantage. From the minute the Wildcats moved into 2,800-seat Alumni Gym, at the corner of South Limestone and Avenue of Champions, opponents found it next to impossible to win there. Kentucky put together a remarkable 247-24 record over 26 seasons at the gym, capping its success with an 84-game home winning streak. Adolph Rupp's teams were 203-8 in 20 seasons there.

The $100,000 structure opened for the 1924-25 season, in response to arguments that the Wildcats' previous home, Buell Armory, was not fit to hold the growing crowds that were flocking to Kentucky games. The UK Board of Trustees approved the construction of a new gym, and the Wildcats celebrated by going 8-2 in their first season in the building.

At first, critics scoffed at the gymnasium's size, saying that it was too large and therefore too costly. But they quickly were proved wrong. Before long, fights broke out as patrons tried to secure choice seating. Also, limitations were placed on student tickets. As the 1950s dawned, it was clear that Kentucky needed a larger arena. But Alumni Gym still stands—for use as a practice facility and some intramural games—offering current UK athletes and students a glimpse of the roots of the UK basketball phenomenon.

memorial coliseum

It was called a "white elephant" by those who believed spending nearly $4 million on an athletic facility was reckless. Imagine, a building with 11,500 seats for basketball. It was preposterous.

In a way, the skeptics were right. By the time UK's Memorial Coliseum was 15 years old, the seating capacity was ridiculous—ridiculously low, that is. Even though the Coliseum was considered grandiose by 1950 standards—the facility opened on December 1 of that year—it soon became a casualty of the overwhelming force of Kentucky basketball. As the Wildcats grew more and more popular within the state and continued to flex their considerable muscle on the national scene, the once-mighty Coliseum became quaint and inadequate. Not that it didn't serve as a brick-and-mortar symbol of the program's great tradition.

From the moment UK began playing there, Memorial Coliseum was a snakepit for opposing teams. Adolph Rupp's Wildcats won their first 45 games at the facility before Georgia Tech sprung a stunning 59-58 upset on January 8, 1955. The setback was difficult for UK fans to accept, but it didn't signal an end to Kentucky's dominance at the Coliseum. In 25 seasons there, Kentucky posted seven perfect home records, lost only one game eight times and fashioned a 306-38 mark overall.

Though Kentucky moved out of the arena after the 1975-76 season, the building still houses the basketball program's offices and weight and locker facilities. And each fall, a capacity crowd packs the Coliseum for the Wildcats' Midnight Madness.

Memorial Coliseum also is the home floor for UK women's basketball, gymnastics and volleyball.

freedom hall

It may seem odd for UK to think of Louisville as homey, but Freedom Hall has been a warm, comfortable place for the Wildcats over the years. Opened in 1957, the building was barely broken in when Kentucky put a blue-and-white stamp on it by capturing the 1958 NCAA title there. The Cats defeated Seattle, 84-72, for the crown.

From that season on, Kentucky has played at least one game per season—with great results—at its "home away from home." The Wildcats are 49-15 at Freedom Hall. UK began playing in Louisville in 1908, and it won 32 consecutive games in the city beginning in 1946.

Freedom Hall, which sits on the grounds of the Kentucky Fair and Exposition Center, has played host to six NCAA championship games. It boasts a seating capacity of 18,865, but on January 3, 1993, 20,060 fans crammed into the arena to watch Kentucky play Indiana. That stood as an attendance record for the facility until March 2, 1996, when 20,076 saw a Louisville-Massachusetts matchup.

rupp arena

Just as Alumni Gym and Memorial Coliseum were considered by some to be too large and expensive for their times, plans for a downtown-Lexington sports palace met some resistance. Though Rupp Arena was to be part of a $53 million Lexington Center complex, which included an exhibition hall, a hotel and a shopping mall, the arena's 23,000-seat capacity was seen as excessive, particularly at a time when most college basketball programs were playing in facilities that held many thousands less.

Yet Kentucky basketball has always been larger than life, so it was fitting that Rupp Arena would be gigantic. And Rupp, which opened in November 1976, remains one of college basketball's most impressive and imposing venues. And just as its predecessors were filled to capacity, Rupp has been the scene of overflow crowds. In 1990-91, UK set a school record by averaging 24,025 fans per game.

There was little doubt about whose name would grace the arena. The legendary Adolph Rupp had been retired for four seasons when the Wildcats moved into their fancy new digs, but he remained a vivid and compelling reminder of the program's glory days. So, the school named the arena in honor of the old coach, who died early in the second season of the building's existence.

The Wildcats have enjoyed tremendous success at Rupp, winning 340 of their 379 games in the arena. UK's home records at Rupp include marks of 18-0, 16-0 (three times), 15-0, 14-0 and 13-0 (twice). Kentucky has won three national championships since moving into Rupp.

The arena played host to the 1985 Final Four, in which Villanova shocked the basketball world by upsetting Georgetown in the title game.

Adolph Rupp acknowledges the crowd during opening ceremonies at the imposing arena named in honor of the legendary coach.

Most Exciting Moments

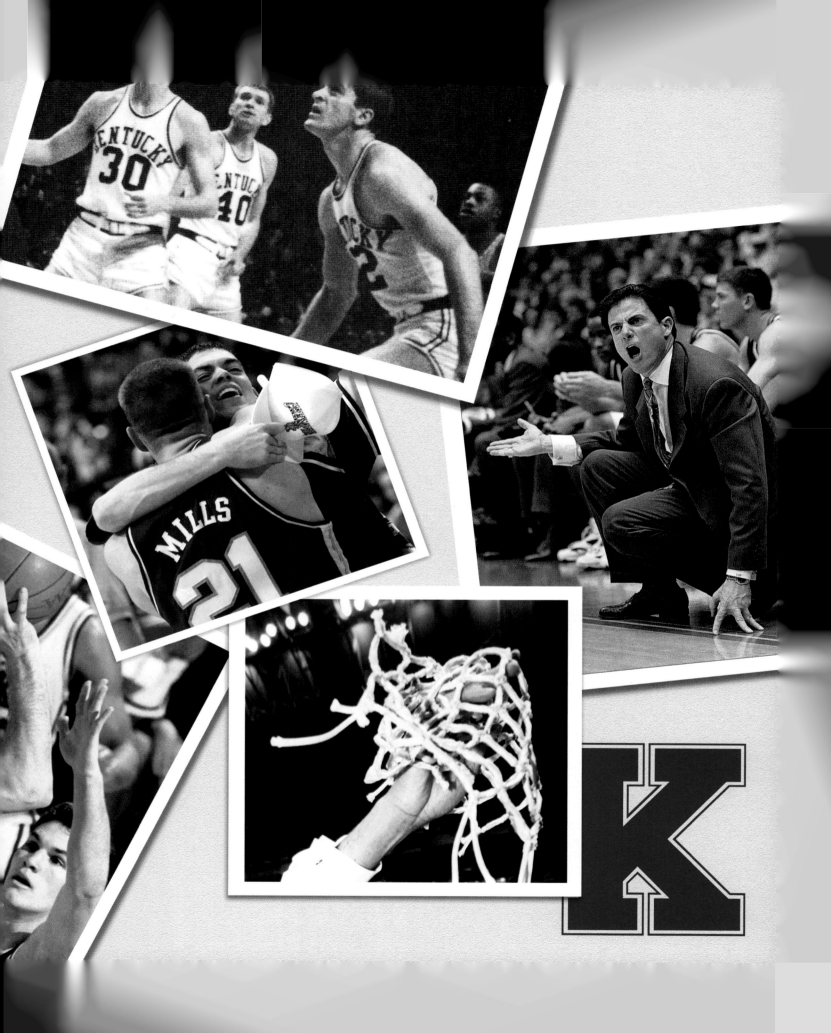

AN UNFORGETTABLE LOSS

The 1992 East Regional final in Philadelphia was an epic struggle between defending NCAA champion Duke and Rick Pitino's Unforgettables, a group that few people considered an elite team. Led by four gritty, low-profile seniors who had weathered the probation years, plus sophomore standout Jamal Mashburn, Kentucky had somehow scratched its way to 29 wins. When Sean Woods hit a shot in the lane against Duke with 2.1 seconds remaining in overtime and a Final Four berth on the line, UK slipped ahead, 103-102. After a timeout, Duke's Grant Hill then fired a baseball pass from the baseline. All-American Christian Laettner caught it, dribbled once, turned and let fly from 17 feet out. Swish. In a flash, ecstasy had turned to agony for UK, a 104-103 loser in perhaps the greatest college basketball game ever played. Yet the pain was almost instantly tempered by a sense of awe over what UK's ultimate overachievers had nearly accomplished.

After taking a baseball pass from Grant Hill in the dying seconds of overtime in the 1992 East Regional final, Duke standout Christian Laettner squared up for a shot over Kentucky's Deron Feldhaus (opposite page). When Laettner let loose with his 17-footer, UK held a 103-102 lead; when the ball nestled into the net, the Wildcats found themselves coping with an agonizing defeat. Meanwhile, the Blue Devils celebrated their good fortune.

JIM-DANDY JIMMY DAN

The Wildcats took a 24-4 record into the 1975 Mideast Regional final against an Indiana team that had compiled a 31-0 record and routed UK by 24 points early in the season. But these weren't the same Hoosiers. All-American Scott May, who scored 25 points against the Cats in the first Indiana-Kentucky meeting, had suffered a late-season arm fracture and was available for only brief duty. Kentucky broke open a taut game and guarded a 10-point lead with 4:22 left. But led by Kent Benson (33 points, 23 rebounds), the Hoosiers rallied within 92-90 with five seconds remaining. Kentucky had the ball; Indiana had the momentum. Enter UK swingman Jimmy Dan Conner, who then salted away matters by dribbling free of Hoosiers for four seconds—for UK, they were four exhilarating ticks on the clock—before being fouled. Conner, who finished with 17 points, missed the free throw, but Indiana couldn't get off another shot. Revitalized after a 13-13 finish in 1973-74, Kentucky was Final Four-bound.

After dribbling away four victory-clinching seconds in the 1975 Mideast Regional final, Kentucky's Jimmy Dan Conner was fouled by Indiana's Wayne Radford. A shoving match ensued (inset) before Conner misfired on his free-throw attempt. No matter. Bob Knight's top-ranked Hoosiers were unable to get off another shot and the Wildcats came away with a 92-90 upset victory.

A FREE THROW FOR PRESTIGE

Adolph Rupp was in his 16th season at Kentucky when freshman Ralph Beard toed the free-throw line with 40 seconds remaining in the 1946 NIT title game. At that juncture, Rupp's teams had won nine SEC championships but had yet to acquire real stature amid the big boys of college basketball. True, the Helms Athletic Foundation conferred best-in-the-land status on the 1932-33 Cats, but that was an unofficial, retroactive honor aimed at determining the elite of college basketball in the pre-NCAA Tournament days. Now, after failing to cart home a title trophy in the 1942 and 1945 NCAA tourneys and the 1944 NIT, UK had a chance to assert itself on the national stage in the then-prestigious NIT. The Cats were tied with Rhode Island, 45-45, at Madison Square Garden when Beard eyed the basket. His shot was true, and the Wildcats held on for the NIT crown—their first "national" title.

UK's Jack Tingle (left) and Rhode Island's Ernie Calverley, whose teams squared off for the 1946 NIT title, got together outside the world-famous New York arena where the tourney was played.

A decisive free throw by Ralph Beard (left) in the late going of the 1946 NIT championship game against Rhode Island thrust Kentucky into the national limelight. Beard scored a game-high 13 points and helped put the clamps on Rams star Calverley (No. 3), guarded in the action above by Wallace "Wah Wah" Jones.

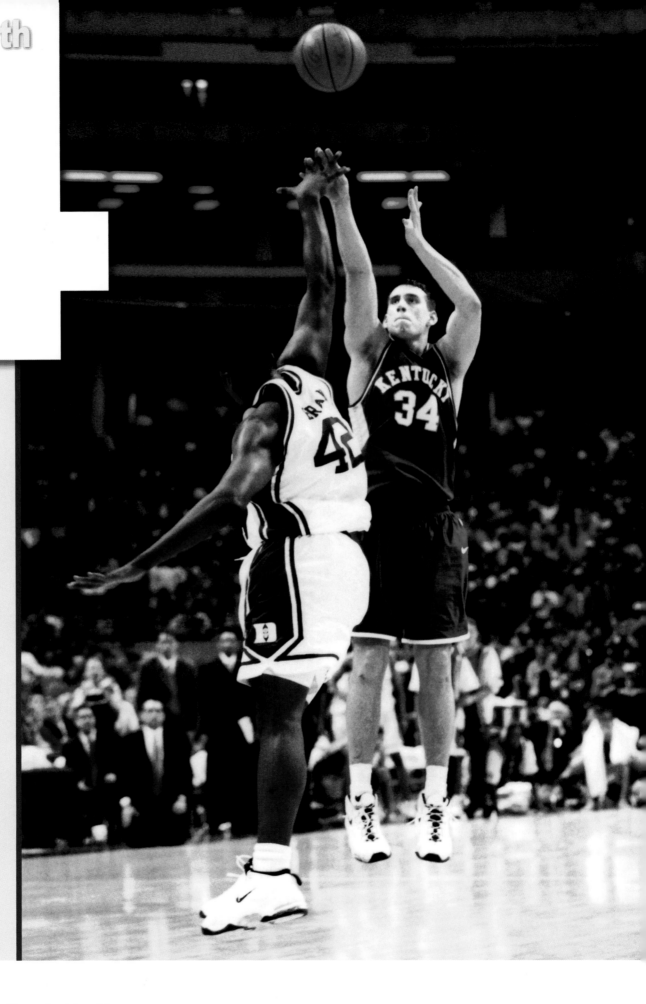

4th

SIX YEARS LATER, REVENGE

It had been six years since Christian Laettner and Duke shattered Kentucky's dreams in an East Regional title game. Still, defeating a new cast of Blue Devils in the 1998 South Regional final would be sweet—if attainable. But with 7:30 remaining in the first half, Kentucky appeared to have the proverbial two chances of winning—slim and none. The Wildcats trailed, 38-20. Despite closing within 10 points at halftime, UK went into another funk and fell behind, 71-54, with 9:38 to play. Then came a 26-8 UK blitz—capped by Cameron Mills' 3-pointer with 2:15 on the clock—that vaulted Kentucky into an 80-79 lead. It was Mills' only field-goal attempt of the game. With 39.4 seconds to go, Scott Padgett's 3-pointer gave UK the lead for good at 84-81. Not that there weren't more anxious moments. With the Wildcats ahead, 86-84, as time ticked down, Duke's William Avery launched a 35-foot prayer. When it went unanswered, UK had seized a very special moment.

With the 1998 South Regional final between Kentucky and Duke deadlocked at 81-81 with 39.4 seconds to play, UK's Scott Padgett lofted a 3-point attempt (opposite page)—and his reaction made it clear that the shot hit the mark. The field goal gave Kentucky the lead for good in a rousing 86-84 win that helped ease the pain of the 1992 "Laettner game." The Wildcats' Cameron Mills, whose 3-pointer with 2:15 remaining had pushed the Cats ahead after they trailed by 17 points earlier in the second half, got a postgame victory hug from teammate Steve Masiello.

5th

DOWN (BY 31), BUT NOT OUT

Kentucky had lost two consecutive games entering its February 15, 1994, clash with LSU at Baton Rouge—and it wasn't long before a third straight defeat seemed inevitable. Even though the Tigers were SEC West also-rans, they ran wild early and built a 68-37 lead over the Wildcats with 15:34 to play. Kentucky then put up a barrage of 3-pointers—the Cats sank 12 of the long-range shots in 23 second-half attempts—and whittled away at the massive deficit. With LSU's edge eventually sliced to 95-90, Tony Delk drilled a 3-pointer with 1:40 to play and Walter McCarty supplied the defining moment by hitting a trey with 19 seconds left to pull UK ahead, 96-95. Scoring the final nine points of the game, UK wound up a highly improbable 99-95 winner. The comeback from a 31-point deficit tied the Division I record (Duke, December 1950) for most points overcome in the second half to win.

Down by 20 points against LSU early in the second half, UK saw the deficit expand to 68-37 in the next 1 minute, 25 seconds, leaving coach Rick Pitino bewildered. But the Wildcats kept their cool and chipped away at the Tigers' lead with an avalanche of 3-pointers and pesky defensive play (exhibited, left photo, by Walter McCarty and Jeff Brassow). With LSU's edge cut to 95-90, the Cats' Tony Delk (No. 00, lower right photo) hit a trey and McCarty followed with a 3-pointer that shot Kentucky into the lead. When the horn sounded—UK outscored LSU 62-27 in the final 15:34 and won 99-95—one Tigers player couldn't bear to look up.

6th

TUBBY'S TITLE

For years, Kentucky was looked upon as one of the last bastions of segregation in big-time college basketball. All that changed in the Joe B. Hall years. Then, in 1997, UK went beyond recruiting black players—it hired an African American head coach, Orlando "Tubby" Smith. In his first season, Smith guided the Wildcats to a 35-4 record and the 1998 NCAA championship. Roaring back from a 10-point halftime deficit in the title game, Smith's Cats exploited a superior bench and an up-tempo game to wear down Utah. Jeff Sheppard's baseline jump shot gave Kentucky the lead for good at 65-64, and the Cats won going away, 78-69. At game's end, Kentucky players hoisted Smith on their shoulders and gave him a victory ride. Holding the championship net aloft, the coach was at the center of a milestone UK moment.

It was sheer ecstasy for Kentucky and coach Tubby Smith as UK players lifted Smith onto their shoulders after the Wildcats defeated Utah in the 1998 NCAA championship game. The Cats, trailing by 10 points at halftime (the largest intermission deficit ever overcome in the title game), used a deep bench and an up-tempo style of play to subdue the Utes. Kentucky seized the lead for good with 4:53 remaining when Jeff Sheppard sank a jump shot (opposite page).

7th

RICK PITINO'S THE ONE

Kentucky's mighty basketball legacy was a shambles. Probation and scandal had made UK an example of all that was negative in college basketball. Coach Eddie Sutton was out after the 1988-89 season, never to be forgiven by some UK supporters. The program needed someone who could win again—with dignity and pride. It needed Rick Pitino. Criticized by some as too slick and viewed by others as a curious choice because of his Northeast pedigree and lack of ties to Kentucky, Pitino nonetheless was the man for the job. When he was introduced as the Wildcats' new coach on June 1, 1989—he had just led the New York Knicks to a division championship—Pitino brought instant energy to the program and renewed confidence as well. With players and fans reinvigorated, Pitino didn't disappoint. He would guide the Cats to three Final Fours and one NCAA title.

It was "meet the press" time on June 1, 1989, when Rick Pitino was introduced as Kentucky's new basketball coach. The hiring of Pitino was a masterstroke for a reeling UK program, which needed a dynamic coach who would restore dignity and pride and, at the same time, carry on the Wildcats' winning tradition. Kentucky athletic director C.M. Newton, who at the time had been on the job only two months, placed a UK pin on the lapel of the successor to Eddie Sutton.

8th

NOT JUST ANOTHER GAME

No Kentucky starter was taller than 6-5. Because of the Wildcats' lack of size—and UK's 15-10 record in the previous season—not much was expected of the 1965-66 team. But these Cats won their first 23 games and rocketed to the top of the wire-service polls. Not even an early-March loss at Tennessee could derail Rupp's Runts, who were led by Pat Riley and Louie Dampier, with Larry Conley, Tommy Kron and Thad Jaracz contributing mightily. The Wildcats subdued Duke in the national semifinals, 83-79, before the magic ended against Don Haskins' Texas Western team in the NCAA title game. Haskins started five black players—in stark contrast to UK's all-white roster—and the Miners prevailed, 72-65. When the final buzzer sounded, it marked more than the end of UK's spirited attempt to win another championship. The game also helped underscore a fundamental change occurring in America, one in which blacks were proving they could thrive and excel in every aspect of society if given an equal opportunity.

It is rare when a basketball game has societal implications, but that was the case in 1966 when Texas Western and Kentucky met for the national championship. At a time when the civil-rights movement was ushering in vast changes in America, the NCAA title game—matching Texas Western's five black starters against a UK team that had an all-white roster—reflected the existing barriers. UK's Thad Jaracz (No. 55), Tommy Kron (30), Larry Conley (40), Pat Riley (42, foreground) and the rest of the Wildcats came up short against the Miners, who defeated Rupp's Runts, 72-65.

9th

THE RETURN

The lights went dark on the Kentucky program in 1952-53 when an NCAA suspension limited the Wildcats to four intrasquad exhibitions. Adolph Rupp stewed at the embarrassment of being shut down because of a gambling scandal. So, when the 1953-54 season dawned against Temple on December 5 at Memorial Coliseum, the coach and his team were eager to reclaim their spot on the national stage. From the emotionally charged moment when the UK players first ran onto the floor to game's end, the visiting Owls encountered a buzz saw. Cliff Hagan, who would lead the team with a 24-point scoring average that season, burned the Owls for 51 points—a school record at the time—and Kentucky rolled to an 86-59 victory. The Cats were back—big time. UK went on to finish 25-0, but Rupp held his team out of the NCAA tournament because of the tourney ineligibility of (left to right, inset) Hagan and fellow graduate students Lou Tsioropoulos and Frank Ramsey.

Emotions ran high—and Cliff Hagan ran hot—on the night of December 5, 1953, when Kentucky returned to intercollegiate basketball action after enduring a one-year suspension. Hagan, driving past Temple's John Kane, went on a 51-point spree on that memorable evening as the fired-up Wildcats pounded the Owls, 86-59, before a packed house at Memorial Coliseum. Adolph Rupp's Cats went on to a perfect season.

THE PERFECT MEDICINE

Top-ranked Kentucky was 31-2 when it met Kansas State for the 1951 NCAA championship, but illness and injury left coach Adolph Rupp with only six fully able-bodied players for the title game in Minneapolis. Kansas State appeared capable of knocking off UK, which was bidding for its third national crown in four seasons. Sure enough, K-State bolted to a 19-13 lead. Rupp then took a chance by calling Cliff Hagan out of sick bay despite the sophomore's fever and sore throat. Hagan provided a spark almost immediately after entering the game, contributing a key tip-in, and he teamed with center Bill Spivey to power a Kentucky resurgence. UK drew within 29-27 at halftime, and it was all UK after intermission. The Cats' defense stiffened, and Spivey asserted himself inside. The 7-footer finished with a game-high 22 points and 21 rebounds. Hagan, the man whose presence seemed to get UK going, wound up with 10 points on five-for-six shooting from the floor. Kentucky won, 68-58.

Kentucky sophomore Cliff Hagan (left photo, hugging teammate Lucian Whitaker) didn't allow a fever and a sore throat to keep him on the sidelines in the 1951 NCAA title game. He got well in a hurry—and so did UK, which needed a boost off the bench after falling behind, 19-13, against Kansas State. After entering the game, Hagan made a key tip-in and then teamed with Bill Spivey to ignite the Cats to a 68-58 victory and their third national crown in four years. UK had reached the final by defeating Illinois, 76-74, in a game in which Spivey (No. 77, above) scored 28 points.

Greatest Performances

JACK GIVENS' 41

Joe B. Hall never forgot the teachings of coaching legend Henry Iba: If a team extends its defense somewhere near halfcourt, something can be exploited in the middle. In Kentucky's 1978 NCAA championship game against Duke, the Blue Devils decided to pressure UK's guards. So, Hall instructed senior forward Jack Givens to patrol the foul-line area. Givens did just that, and he found hole after hole in Duke's zone. By halftime, Givens had 23 points—including Kentucky's last 16 of the first 20 minutes. Duke was more attentive to Givens in the second half, but "Goose" nonetheless tacked on 18 more points. Overall, he sank 18 of 27 field-goal attempts, most from about 15 feet out, en route to a stirring 41-point night. When James Lee slammed home one of his thunder dunks in the final seconds, Kentucky had a 94-88 victory and the national title.

Repeatedly finding holes in Duke's zone, Kentucky's Jack Givens (No. 21) shot holes in that defensive alignment in the 1978 NCAA championship game. By game's end, "Goose" had 41 points and the Wildcats had their first national title since 1958. Givens, who was named the Most Outstanding Player in the Final Four, capped a big night in St. Louis with the celebratory honor of cutting down the net.

2nd

876 WINS, 4 NCAA TITLES

To many people, Adolph Rupp *is* Kentucky basketball. Though born in Kansas, Rupp became the dominant image of the UK program. His 876 career victories stood as the Division I standard for 25 years, until North Carolina's Dean Smith edged past Rupp's total. When Rupp arrived in Lexington in 1930, Wildcats basketball was a reasonably successful regional concern. Rupp made it a national enterprise. His Cats won four NCAA championships—three of them in a four-year span—and captured an NIT title. They also had an undefeated season and won 27 Southeastern Conference crowns. From 1943-44 through 1954-55, Rupp's teams compiled an astounding 305-29 record. Though criticized for his reluctance to recruit black players, Rupp was a giant of his time. The legend of Kentucky basketball is built on the performances of many great players, but none was as influential, important or successful as Rupp.

Admiring new hardware for the UK trophy case became a regular occurrence for Adolph Rupp. As his players looked on in March 1949, Rupp accepted the award for the Wildcats' second consecutive NCAA championship. Besides coaching the Cats to national titles in 1948 and '49, the Baron of the Bluegrass also directed Kentucky to NCAA crowns in 1951 and 1958. He won 876 games and lost 190 in his 41 seasons in Lexington. In a six-season span starting in 1945-46, Rupp's UK teams won three NCAA titles and one NIT championship. In the two other seasons in that time frame, the Cats compiled 34-3 and 25-5 records.

3rd

A FABULOUS SEASON

The 10th NCAA Tournament was held in 1948. The roll of previous champions started with Oregon in 1939 and ended with Holy Cross in 1947. Kentucky was nowhere to be found. But on March 23, 1948, in New York, the Wildcats etched their names onto the list. The starters are burned into the minds of every serious UK fan: Ralph Beard, Alex Groza, Wah Wah Jones, Kenny Rollins and Cliff Barker. The Fabulous Five, with support from Jim Line, Dale Barnstable and Joe Holland, went 36-3 under Adolph Rupp, who was in his 18th season at UK. Groza handled the inside, Beard ran the team and Jones did just about everything. The crowning achievement: a 58-42 thumping of Baylor in the national title game. That summer, the Fabulous Five was a key part of the U.S. team that brought home Olympic gold from London.

After powering Kentucky to the heights of college basketball in the 1947-48 season—the Cats won their first NCAA crown and set a still-standing school record with 36 victories—the Fabulous Five embarked on an encore performance of excellence. After boarding a liner bound for London and the '48 Olympic Games, UK stars (left to right) Cliff Barker, Wallace "Wah Wah" Jones, Kenny Rollins, Ralph Beard and Alex Groza soon helped the U.S. team win the gold medal. Groza led the Americans with an 11.1-point average and Jones scored 7.2 points per game, helping the United States to an 8-0 record.

129 IN A ROW—
YES, 129

It started quietly enough, on January 4, 1943, with a 64-30 run-through of in-state opponent Fort Knox at Alumni Gym. Twelve years and three national championships later, it ended with a 59-58 loss to lightly regarded Georgia Tech. What it was, was the Wildcats' almost-inconceivable 129-game home-court winning streak. Some of UK's greatest players were part of the record Division I streak—Alex Groza, Ralph Beard, Wah Wah Jones, Bill Spivey, Frank Ramsey and Cliff Hagan. The first 84 wins came at Alumni Gym, the last 45 at Memorial Coliseum. When Kentucky lost to Georgia Tech on January 8, 1955—5-9 Joe Helms delivered the game-winning shot and led all scorers with 23 points—shocked UK fans sat silent in the Coliseum for several minutes. The defeat also ended the longest overall winning streak in Kentucky history at 32 games. The closest any team has come to UK's home-floor streak? That distinction belongs to St. Bonaventure, which won 99 in a row at home (1948-1961).

Before taking on Xavier of Ohio on January 4, 1954, Adolph Rupp and his players were feted with a cake that noted the 11th anniversary of the start of Kentucky's home-court winning streak, which at that point had reached 115 games. The Wildcats defeated the Musketeers, 77-71. A little more than a year later, the streak would end at 129 games when the Cats were dealt a stunning 59-58 defeat by then-SEC rival Georgia Tech.

5th

DAN ISSEL
VS.
THE PISTOL

When Kentucky visited LSU on February 21, 1970, it was the final matchup between scintillating Tigers guard Pete Maravich and UK legend Dan Issel. All Pistol Pete had done in five previous games against the Wildcats was average 49.6 points. Two weeks before this last marquee meeting, Issel had established a UK record with a 53-point salvo against Mississippi. A classic shootout was expected—and Issel and Maravich didn't disappoint. Maravich launched 42 shots and made 23, and he converted 18 of 22 free-throw attempts. *Sixty-four* points. Kentucky, knowing beforehand that it was a deeper team, needed a big but not Herculean game from Issel to counter whatever Pistol Pete might do. And the "Horse" went out and made 19 of 33 floor shots and 13 of 17 foul shots. His 51 points and 17 rebounds, plus 27 points from Mike Pratt and 18 from Tom Parker, led UK to a 121-105 victory.

Louisiana State star Pete Maravich's sleight of hand and scoring prowess dazzled Dan Issel and the Wildcats on February 21, 1970, but Issel had a sensational game, too. Maravich, who earlier in February had established an LSU record with 69 points against Alabama, got 64 against Kentucky and flashed his trademark ballhandling wizardry. Issel countered with 51 points and 17 rebounds—which, combined with solid contributions from his teammates, helped a superior UK team come away with a 16-point victory in Baton Rouge.

6th

TONY'S TREYS TRIP SYRACUSE

No one made more 3-point field goals in Kentucky history than Tony Delk. He came to Kentucky with the range and the eye to be a great outside shooter. Playing in Rick Pitino's system, which preached the press, the break and the long ball, the opportunities would be there. In Delk's final game as a Wildcat, he turned in his best clutch performance from behind the arc. It was the 1996 NCAA title game, and Kentucky needed some firepower to fend off pesky Syracuse. Delk provided it. On a night when the Wildcats shot poorly overall (38.4 percent from the field), Delk drilled seven of his 12 attempts from 3-point range and finished with 24 points. Ron Mercer contributed three treys and 20 points. The Cats wound up with a 76-67 victory and their first national championship in 18 years.

Kentucky's double zero, Tony Delk, was able to zero in from 3-point range in the 1996 NCAA championship game against Syracuse, drilling seven of 12 shots from beyond the arc. With the Wildcats shooting poorly overall, the marksmanship of the senior guard proved crucial as UK nailed down its sixth national title.

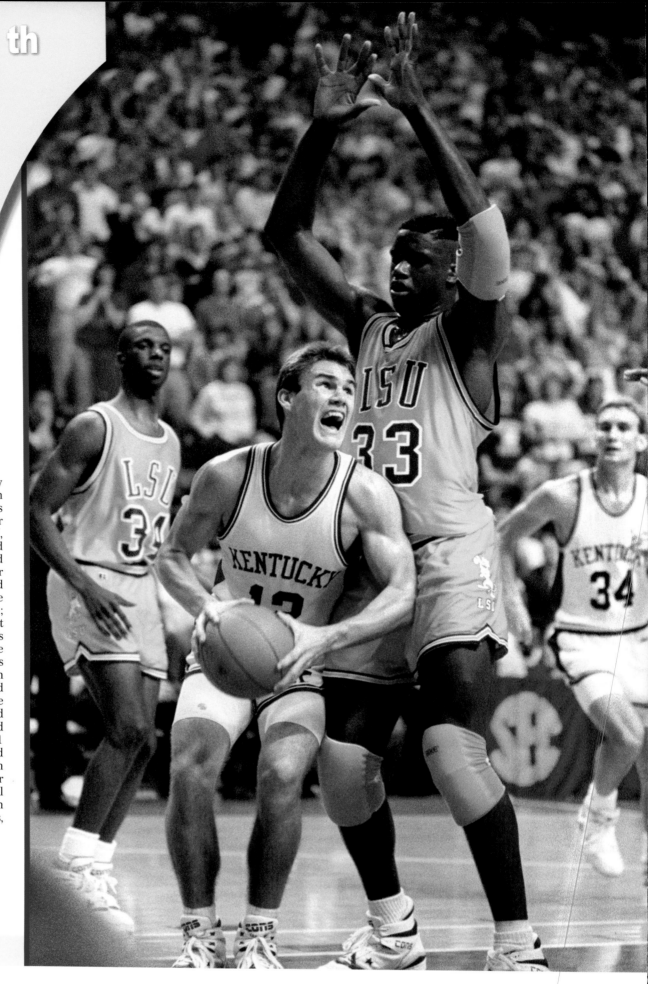

A REVIVAL MEETING AT RUPP

Kentucky vs. LSU, February 15, 1990. Rick Pitino's first team was reeling from NCAA sanctions imposed because of another regime's transgressions. LSU, ranked No. 9 by the Associated Press, featured mercurial guard Chris Jackson and the interior tandem of Shaquille O'Neal and Stanley Roberts. The Tigers were headed for a 23-victory season; Kentucky would finish 14-14. But one of UK's wins came in this thriller at Rupp Arena, and the outcome energized UK players and fans at a time when both needed some sign that good times might be ahead. The Wildcats bolted to a 41-18 lead and led by 12 at halftime. Behind Jackson, who finished with 41 points, LSU stormed back and pulled within two points with 1:12 to play. But Richie Farmer sank six free throws in the final 65 seconds and Kentucky, which had six scorers in double figures, held on for a 100-95 victory.

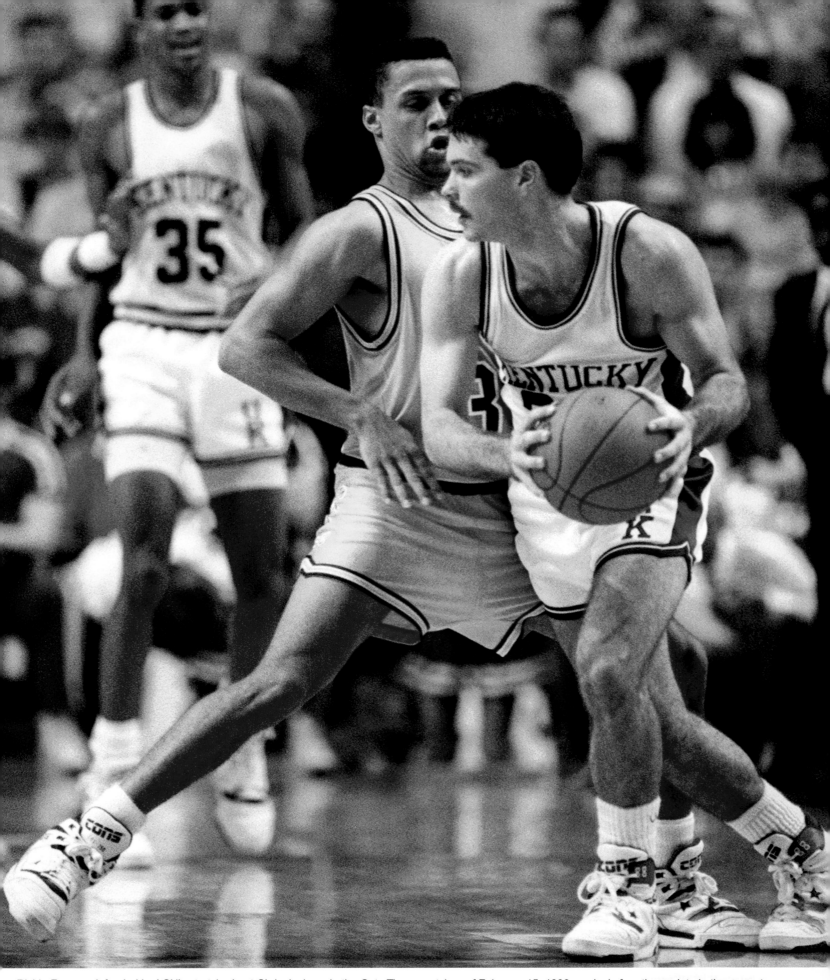

Richie Farmer, defended by LSU's stretched-out Chris Jackson in the Cats-Tigers matchup of February 15, 1990, sank six free throws late in the game to seal UK's upset victory over an LSU team that featured Jackson, Shaquille O'Neal and Stanley Roberts. Derrick Miller scored 29 points for Kentucky and Deron Feldhaus, despite the intimidating presence of O'Neal (No. 33, left photo), added 24 in a stirring win that did wonders for a UK program that was in its first season under the direction of Rick Pitino. John Pelphrey (34) and Reggie Hanson (35) were other Wildcats visible in the spirited action at Rupp Arena.

8th

UK's 2,138-POINT MACHINE

Three seasons in Lexington were enough to make center Dan Issel the Wildcats' all-time leading scorer with 2,138 points. With freshman eligibility still six years away when he entered UK, Issel made his varsity debut as a sophomore in 1967-68 and averaged 16.4 points. He rounded into form late that season with 28 points against Alabama, 31 vs. Georgia and 36 in an NCAA tourney game against Marquette. After a 26.6 average as a junior—a season in which he scored 35 or more points five times—Issel concluded his career in 1969-70 with a school-record 33.9 points per game. He reached 40 or more points eight times as a senior, setting a Wildcats record with 53 points at Ole Miss on February 7, 1970, when he sank 23 of 34 field-goal attempts and all seven of his foul shots. For good measure, Issel pulled down 19 rebounds against the Rebels.

Dan Issel always had his game face on. The big man from Batavia, Ill., averaged a school-record 33.9 points as a senior, a year in which he scored 40 or more points eight times. Issel set a Kentucky mark that season with 53 points against Ole Miss, poured in 51 against LSU, netted 47 against Alabama and got 44 in an NCAA Tournament game against Notre Dame. From the midpoint of his sophomore season through the rest of his UK career, he was a double-figure scorer in 69 consecutive games. In one four-game stretch in his final year, he averaged 43.8 points. Issel twice powered the Wildcats within one victory of the Final Four.

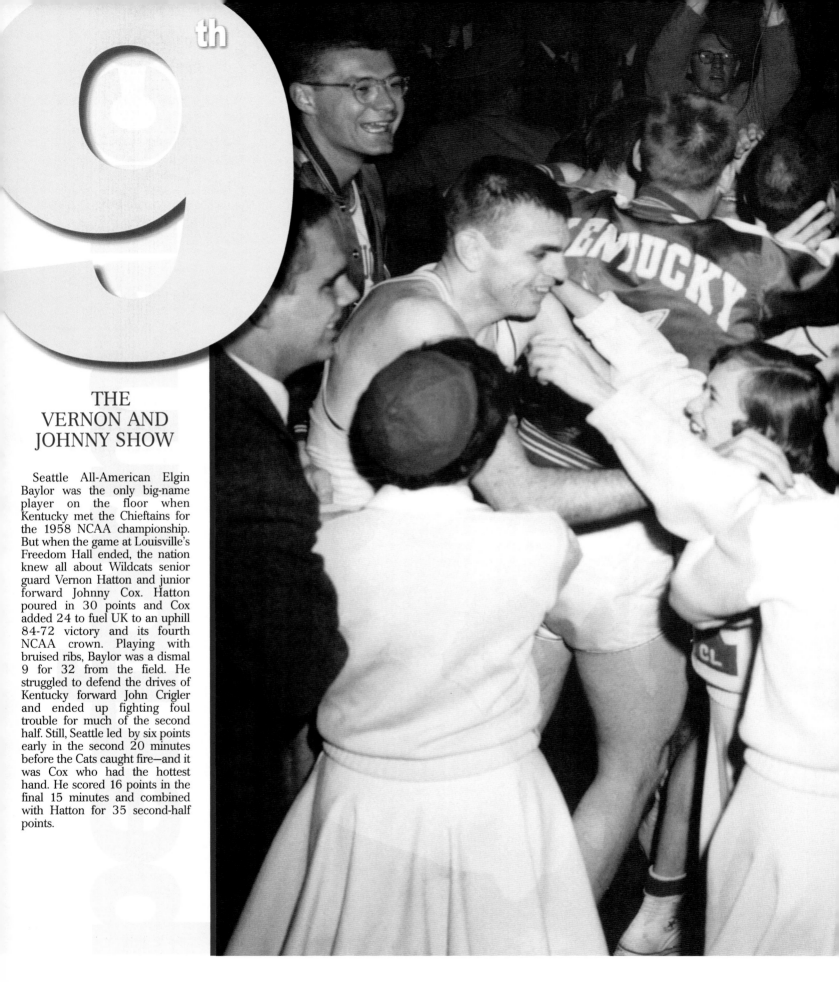

9th

THE VERNON AND JOHNNY SHOW

Seattle All-American Elgin Baylor was the only big-name player on the floor when Kentucky met the Chieftains for the 1958 NCAA championship. But when the game at Louisville's Freedom Hall ended, the nation knew all about Wildcats senior guard Vernon Hatton and junior forward Johnny Cox. Hatton poured in 30 points and Cox added 24 to fuel UK to an uphill 84-72 victory and its fourth NCAA crown. Playing with bruised ribs, Baylor was a dismal 9 for 32 from the field. He struggled to defend the drives of Kentucky forward John Crigler and ended up fighting foul trouble for much of the second half. Still, Seattle led by six points early in the second 20 minutes before the Cats caught fire—and it was Cox who had the hottest hand. He scored 16 points in the final 15 minutes and combined with Hatton for 35 second-half points.

The big-game play of guard Vernon Hatton and forward Johnny Cox contributed in no small way to a joyous scene at Freedom Hall in Louisville on March 22, 1958. Hatton and Cox had just combined for 54 Kentucky points, helping the Wildcats rally past Seattle in the NCAA title game. The Cats got Chieftains superstar Elgin Baylor into foul trouble and hounded him overall, with Ed Beck (No. 34, inset) applying sizable pressure on the All-American at one point. Baylor shot poorly, yet finished with strong numbers (25 points, 19 rebounds).

10th

ALEX THE GREAT

Alex Groza played less than 30 minutes in the 1949 NCAA championship game, but that was enough to carry Kentucky to its second consecutive national crown. Groza, a powerful 6-7 center who averaged 20.5 points in the '48-'49 season, broke loose for 25 points in the title game against Oklahoma A&M. He scored more than half of UK's points—the Wildcats won, 46-36—and finished with twice as many points as the game's No. 2 scorer, the Aggies' Jack Shelton, who had 12. No other UK player had more than five points. Aggies coach Henry Iba assigned lean Bob Harris to cover Groza, but Harris was overmatched. Groza had 15 points in the first 20 minutes, and he added 10 in the second half despite missing playing time because of foul trouble and eventually drawing his fifth violation. The big man finished with as many field goals (nine) as the entire Aggies team.

Sandwiched between two Oklahoma A&M players in the 1949 NCAA championship game, Kentucky center Alex Groza wound up putting the squeeze on coach Henry Iba's Oklahomans. He burned A&M for 25 points, finishing with as many field goals (nine) as the entire Aggies team, as UK won its second consecutive national title. Groza, who earlier in his career had posed for a publicity photo without his familiar No. 15, was sensational in the Wildcats' other two games in the '49 NCAA Tournament, scoring 30 points against Villanova and 27 against Illinois.

Cats Chronology

In its early days, the University of Kentucky was known by such names as the Agricultural and Mechanical College of Kentucky, Kentucky State College and Kentucky State University. Regardless of the time frame, the university and its athletic teams are referred to as Kentucky, UK, Wildcats or Cats throughout the chronology. (Note: The name "University of Kentucky" became official in 1916.)

1902-03

Record: 1-2. In the first basketball game in University of Kentucky history, UK loses to in-state opponent Georgetown, 15-6, on Feb. 6, 1903. ... The school's first victory comes against the Lexington YMCA team.

1903-04

1-4. The lone triumph is over Cincinnati.

1904-05

1-4. Three of UK's five games are against Lexington-based "Kentucky University," which later becomes Transylvania University. UK scores only one point in one of those games.

1905-06

5-9. In a low-scoring era, UK loses its final three games by a total of 76 points.

1906-07

3-6. The three wins come in a stretch of four games.

1907-08

5-6. For the first time, UK scores in double figures in every game.

1908-09

5-4. Kentucky is assured of its first winning record after defeating Cincinnati in the next-to-last game of the season.

1909-10

4-8. In the fall, UK athletic teams become known as the Wildcats. ... Kentucky wins its first two games, then drops six straight.

1910-11

5-6. The Wildcats, showing signs of better times ahead, end the season with a four-game winning streak.

1911-12

9-0. UK concludes a perfect season with a one-point win over Georgetown (Ky.), a team it had defeated by 29 points in the season opener.

1912-13

5-3. The Wildcats play Louisville for the first time, roll to a 34-10 victory.

1913-14

12-2. Kentucky closes the season with an 8-0 run.

1914-15

7-5. The season deteriorates after a 4-0 start.

1915-16

8-6. D.W. Hart becomes the first player in recorded UK basketball history to post a double-digit scoring average, 13.3.

1916-17

4-6. Hopes of a .500-or-better season evaporate with two season-ending losses at Tennessee.

1917-18

9-2-1. A scorer's error results in a tie game with Kentucky Wesleyan.

1918-19

6-8. There is no scorer's error in the season opener against Kentucky Wesleyan—the Wildcats win, 46-5.

1919-20

5-7. Sophomore Basil Hayden averages 10.8 points.

1920-21

13-1. Hayden is the first UK player to make an All-American team. ... The Cats win the Southern Conference title by edging Georgia, 20-19, on a free throw by Bill King.

1921-22

10-6. Kentucky posts consecutive double-figure victory totals for the first time.

1922-23

3-10. A nine-game losing streak makes for a long season.

1923-24

13-3. The Cats do an about-face, win nine consecutive games.

1924-25

13-8. UK's Alumni Gymnasium opens. The Wildcats defeat Cincinnati in the first game played in the 2,800-seat facility.

1925-26

15-3. Kentucky sandwiches a 15-game winning streak between two season-opening losses and a season-ending defeat.

1926-27

3-13. A sign of trouble: UK's leading scorer, Paul Jenkins, averages only 6.1 points.

1927-28

12-6. For the first time, the Cats have two players with double-figure scoring averages: Irvine Jeffries (11.5) and Cecil Combs (10.3).

1928-29

12-5. UK plays a three-overtime game against Miami of Ohio, wins 43-42.

1929-30

16-3. In his third and last season as UK coach, John Mauer guides the Wildcats to a school-record victory total.

1930-31

15-3. **Adolph Rupp**, a high school coach in Freeport, Ill., becomes Kentucky coach. In Rupp's first game at UK, the Wildcats overwhelm Georgetown (Ky.), 67-19.

1931-32

15-2. Forest "Aggie" Sale is UK's first consensus All-American basketball player.

1932-33

21-3. This Kentucky team is declared the national champion by the Helms Athletic Foundation. ... Sale again is a consensus All-American. ... The Wildcats capture the first title in the newly formed Southeastern Conference by winning the league tournament. ... The Cats post their first 20-win season and go 8-0 in the SEC.

1933-34

16-1. Kentucky finishes 11-0 in the SEC. ... UK pushes a two-season winning streak to 24 games before losing to Florida in the SEC Tournament.

1934-35

19-2. The Cats' Leroy Edwards is a consensus All-American. ...

Kentucky is 11-0 in the SEC. ... UK plays in Madison Square Garden for the first time, loses to New York University by one point.

1935-36

15-6. The six losses are a UK high in six seasons under Rupp.

1936-37

17-5. A 5-3 SEC record is good for only a tie for fifth place, but the Wildcats win the conference tournament.

1937-38

13-5. Joe Hagan's shot from near midcourt beats Marquette. ... Three of the five losses come in succession on a trip to Michigan State, Detroit and Notre Dame.

1938-39

16-4. After a shaky January—they suffer all four of their losses in a five-game stretch that month—the Wildcats rebound to win their final eight regular-season games and then take the SEC Tournament crown with victories over Mississippi, LSU and Tennessee.

1939-40

15-6. After Vanderbilt and Tennessee deal Kentucky two of its regular-season losses, UK defeats the Commodores and the Volunteers in the SEC Tournament before downing Georgia for the tourney title.

1940-41

17-8. Nonconference play takes it toll as Kentucky loses to

Nebraska, Creighton, Indiana, Notre Dame, West Virginia and Xavier. The other defeats are inflicted by Tennessee, which beats the Cats in mid-January and again in the SEC Tournament championship game.

1944-45

22-4. The Cats win their first 11 games, one of them a 75-6 annihilation of Arkansas State. ... Freshman sensation **Alex Groza** scores 77 points in one three-game stretch, but the 6-7 center enters military service after appearing in only 10 games. He misses the rest of the season and all of 1945-46. ... In the NCAA tourney, Ohio State eliminates Kentucky from the title hunt.

1945-46

28-2. Kentucky wins the NIT title with victories over Arizona, West Virginia and Rhode Island. ... The only losses of the season are to Temple and Notre Dame. ... The Wildcats win their final 15 games. ... Despite UK's dominance, only one Wildcat finishes with a double-figure scoring average, guard Jack Parkinson (11.3).

1941-42

19-6. UK makes its first appearance in the NCAA Tournament, loses to Dartmouth, 47-28, in the Eastern final after edging Illinois.

1942-43

17-6. For the second time in three years, the Wildcats lose to Tennessee in the SEC Tournament final. ... Kentucky defeats Fort Knox, 64-30, on Jan. 4 at Alumni Gym, begins a home-court winning streak that will last 12 years.

1943-44

19-2. UK's Bob Brannum is a consensus All-American. ... The Wildcats lose to St. John's in the NIT semifinals, then beat Oklahoma A&M in the third-place game.

1946-47

34-3. Kentucky loses to Utah in the NIT championship game. ... The Wildcats' Groza and Ralph Beard are consensus All-Americans. ... The All-SEC Tournament first team is made up entirely of Cats—Beard, Kenny Rollins, Wah Wah Jones, Jack Tingle and Joe Holland. Groza makes the second team. ... The Cats go 11-0 in the SEC. ... UK averages 68.5 points. Opponents score 38.3 per game.

1947-48

36-3. UK wins its first NCAA championship. The Wildcats defeat Baylor in the final after earlier victories over Columbia and Holy Cross. ... Beard again is a consensus All-American. ... Beard makes a 52-foot shot against Tennessee as the first-half clock winds down. ... The Cats go 9-0 in the SEC. ... The U.S. team, with five UK players playing prominent roles, wins the Olympic Games gold medal with an eight-game sweep of the competition. Groza averages a team-high 11.1 points for the United States and Jones scores 7.2 points per game. Rupp is an associate coach for the American squad.

1948-49

32-2. Kentucky repeats as the NCAA champion. The Cats defeat Oklahoma A&M in the final after earlier wins over Villanova and Illinois. ... Beard is a consensus All-American for the third consecutive season; Groza is honored for the second time. ... The Wildcats go 13-0 in the SEC. ... UK compiles a 21-game winning streak. ... The first-ever college basketball poll is released in mid-January. The Associated Press rankings list Saint Louis, Kentucky and Western Kentucky 1-2-3. ... Kentucky loses to Loyola of Chicago in the NIT, then joins the NCAA tourney field. ... Cliff Barker sinks a shot estimated at 63 feet-plus against Vanderbilt. ... Beard and Jones are All-SEC selections for the fourth consecutive season.

1949-50

25-5. The Cats are embarrassed by CCNY, 89-50, in the NIT quarterfinals. ... In its final game at Alumni Gym, Kentucky defeats Vanderbilt, 70-66. It is UK's 84th consecutive victory at the facility.

1950-51

32-2. UK wins the NCAA crown with a victory over Kansas State. Earlier tourney victims: Louisville, St. John's and Illinois. ...

It was ship ahoy for UK's 1948 Olympic Games contingent, which was bound for London. Front, left to right: Wah Wah Jones, Cliff Barker and Ralph Beard. Back, left to right: Kenny Rollins, Adolph Rupp (who assisted U.S. coach Bud Browning), fan Gertrude Fisher and Alex Groza. The entire U.S. squad is at right.

Kentucky fans were disbelieving in October 1951 when former UK players were brought before authorities in New York in connection with a gambling scandal that rocked the college game.

The Wildcats move into 11,500-seat Memorial Coliseum. ... In Kentucky's fourth game at the Coliseum, Rupp defeats his mentor as the Wildcats rout Phog Allen's Kansas team, 68-39. ... Bill Spivey, with averages of 19.2 points and 17.2 rebounds, is a consensus All-American. ... The Cats are 14-0 in the SEC. ... UK reels off a 21-game winning streak.

1951-52

29-3. In October, former Kentucky players are implicated in a far-reaching college basketball gambling scandal. ... Kentucky's **Cliff Hagan** is a consensus All-American. ... The Cats again go 14-0 in the SEC. ... UK wins 23 consecutive games. ... St. John's ousts Kentucky from the NCAA tourney.

1952-53

0-0. Because of NCAA infractions dating to 1948, the Kentucky basketball program is suspended for one season.

1953-54

25-0. UK is the Helms Athletic Foundation's national champion. ... The Wildcats return to

basketball competition on Dec. 5, against Temple, and Hagan scores 51 points in an 86-59 win. ... Hagan averages 24 points and is a consensus All-American for the second time. ... The Cats go 14-0 in the SEC. ... **Cawood Ledford** becomes the radio voice of the Wildcats. ... With its leading players ineligible for the NCAA Tournament because of their status as graduate students, Kentucky declines to play in the tourney.

Cawood Ledford took over as the radio voice of Wildcats basketball in the 1953-54 season. He called games for a rapt statewide audience for nearly four decades.

1954-55

23-3. Georgia Tech ends Kentucky's 129-game home-court winning streak (a still-standing national record), edging the Wildcats, 59-58, on Jan. 8 at Memorial Coliseum. The defeat also ends the longest overall winning streak in UK history at 32 games.

1955-56

20-6. Kentucky's Bob Burrow scores 50 points against LSU. ... The Wildcats score a UK-record 143 points against Georgia—and win by a school-best 77 points. ... Burrow matches Spivey's school mark for rebounds in one game, collecting 34 against Temple.

Cotton Nash had a memorable first season in a UK uniform, averaging 23.4 points in 1961-62.

1956-57

23-5. The Cats lose twice in three games in mid-December nonconference play but win 13 of their next 14 games.

1957-58

23-6. Kentucky wins the NCAA championship. After defeating Miami of Ohio, Notre Dame and Temple, the Wildcats upend Seattle in the title game. ... In Kentucky's third game of the regular season, Vernon Hatton makes a 47-foot shot at the end of the first overtime to tie Temple (an eventual UK opponent in the Final Four). The Cats go on to subdue the Owls in three overtimes.

1958-59

24-3. UK's Johnny Cox is a consensus All-American. ... The defending national champion Cats lose to Louisville in the NCAA Mideast Regional semifinals.

1959-60

18-7. The Wildcats finish third in the SEC, miss the NCAA Tournament.

1960-61

19-9. A January skid of four setbacks in five games sends Kentucky reeling toward a nine-defeat season, the highest loss total to date under Rupp.

1961-62

23-3. UK goes 13-1 in the SEC. ... For the second consecutive season, the Wildcats are eliminated from the NCAA tourney by Ohio State, losing again in the Mideast Regional final. ... **Cotton Nash** averages 23.4 points.

1962-63

16-9. The Wildcats' winning percentage (.640) is the lowest in 36 years.

1963-64

21-6. UK's Nash averages 24 points and is a consensus All-American.

1964-65

15-10. Louie Dampier, **Pat Riley**, Tommy Kron, John Adams and Larry Conley all post double-figure scoring averages. ... After UK's Jan. 23 loss to Florida, the Cats' record stands at 8-7. Kentucky then wins its next five games. ... UK finishes in fifth place in the SEC with a 10-6 record.

1965-66

27-2. The Wildcats play for the NCAA title, lose to Texas Western, 72-65. The game is viewed on sociological as well as athletic terms—the victorious Miners start five black players against a UK team with an all-white roster. The Cats reach the NCAA final with tourney wins over Dayton, Michigan and Duke. ... Kentucky goes 15-1 in the SEC. ... UK wins its first 23 games of the season.

1966-67

13-13. Starters Dampier, Riley and Thad Jaracz return from the standout '65-'66 team but UK experiences its first non-winning

Marquette in the NCAA Mideast Regional semifinals. ... **Dan Issel** averages 26.6 points. ... Harry Lancaster serves his 23rd and last season as a full-time assistant coach under Rupp.

1969-70

26-2. In NCAA Mideast Regional shootouts, Kentucky defeats Notre Dame, 109-99, but loses to Jacksonville, 106-100. ... Issel averages a UK-record 33.9 points and is a consensus All-American. ... Issel scores a school-best 53 points against Mississippi on Feb. 7. Two weeks later, he gets 51 against LSU but is outscored by Pete Maravich. Maravich's 64 points aren't enough, though. Kentucky wins, 121-105. ... The Cats go 17-1 in the SEC.

1970-71

22-6. **Tom Payne** becomes UK's first black basketball player. He averages 16.9 points and 10.1 rebounds. ... The Wildcats are 16-2 in the SEC. ... In the schools' first-ever meeting, Western Kentucky routs UK, 107-83, in the NCAA Mideast Regional semifinals.

season since 1926-27. ... The Cats avoid a losing record by defeating Alabama in their final game. ... Rupp becomes the winningest Division I coach in history with his 760th victory, achieved as Kentucky defeats Mississipp State in Starkville on Feb. 18. He moves past longtime Western Kentucky coach Ed Diddle.

1971-72

21-7. In Rupp's last game as Kentucky coach, the Wildcats lose to Florida State, 73-54, in the NCAA Mideast Regional final in Dayton, Ohio. ... In the Mideast semifinals, Rupp wins his 876th and last game as the Cats defeat Marquette, 85-69. ... Center Jim Andrews is the leading scorer (21.5 average) on Rupp's last team. ... Joe B. Hall, an assistant to Rupp, is named UK coach.

1967-68

22-5. NCAA tourney nemesis Ohio State again bounces UK from the Big Dance. This time, in the Mideast Regional final played on the Wildcats' home floor, the Buckeyes come away 82-81 winners.

1972-73

20-8. In Hall's first game as coach, Kentucky defeats Michigan State, 75-66, at East Lansing.

1968-69

23-5. UK finishes 16-2 in the SEC. ... The Wildcats lose to

1973-74

13-13. In his second year as UK coach, **Hall** matches the worst record ever compiled by a Rupp-coached Wildcats team. ... The Cats suffer four consecutive SEC losses in February, wind up 9-9 in conference play.

1974-75

26-5. UK loses the NCAA title game to UCLA, 92-85. The game marks the end of the coaching career of the Bruins' John Wooden. ... Indiana, with a record of 31-0, falls to Kentucky, 92-90, in the Mideast Regional championship game. ... Kevin Grevey averages more than 20 points for the second straight season, finishing at 23.6.

1975-76

20-10. The Wildcats defeat UNC Charlotte for the NIT crown. UK reaches the title game with wins over Niagara, Kansas State and Providence. ... Jack Givens averages 20.1 points as the leader of a promising sophomore group that includes Mike Phillips, Rick Robey and James Lee.

1976-77

26-4. The Cats move into Rupp Arena, defeat Wisconsin in the first game played in the 23,000-seat facility. ... Kentucky is 16-2 in the SEC. ... UK begins the season 6-0, later has a 14-game winning streak. ... Kentucky scores NCAA Tournament wins over

Mike Flynn (No. 24) made nine of 13 field-goal attempts and scored 22 points in the Wildcats' win over previously unbeaten Indiana in the 1975 Mideast Regional final. Other Cats are Kevin Grevey (35), Bob Guyette (45) and Rick Robey (53).

Rick Robey was riding high after his 20 points and 11 rebounds helped the Wildcats stop Duke in the 1978 NCAA title game.

Princeton and VMI but falls to North Carolina in the East Regional final.

1977-78

30-2. Kentucky wins the NCAA title. The Wildcats reach the final with victories over Florida State, Miami of Ohio, Michigan State and Arkansas. In the championship game, UK stops Duke, 94-88, as Givens scores 41 points. ... The Cats go 16-2 in the SEC. ... Robey sets a Wildcats record for field-goal accuracy, making 63.5 percent of his shots. ... Rupp dies on Dec. 10, 1977. On the same day, No. 1-ranked Kentucky wins at Kansas, where Rupp was a student of the game under the sport's founder, Dr. James Naismith, and coach Phog Allen.

1978-79

19-12. UK makes its seventh appearance in the NIT, loses a first-round game to Clemson in overtime. The game, played at Rupp Arena, draws an NIT-record crowd of 23,522 fans. ... The Cats overcome a six-point deficit in the final 31 seconds of overtime and defeat Kansas, 67-66, at Rupp in the third game of the season.

1979-80

29-6. Kentucky's **Kyle Macy** is a consensus All-American. ... After a season-opening loss to Duke, UK wins 12 in a row. ... Duke strikes again in the NCAA Tournament, edging Kentucky, 55-54, in the Mideast Regional semifinals.

1980-81

22-6. The Cats are upset by Alabama-Birmingham in a second-round game of the NCAA Tournament. The loss comes on the heels of UK's one-and-out showing in the SEC tourney.

1981-82

22-8. UK is shocked again in the NCAA Tournament. This time, Middle Tennessee State sends the Cats packing with an opening-round 50-44 upset.

1982-83

23-8. The Wildcats play rivals Indiana and Louisville in the NCAA Mideast Regional semifinals and final. UK slips past Indiana, 64-59, but loses to Louisville, 80-68, in overtime.

1983-84

29-5. Melvin Turpin, Sam Bowie and Kenny Walker fuel UK's march to the Final Four, where the Wildcats take a 29-22 halftime lead against Georgetown in the national semifinals. But Kentucky turns stone-cold in the second half—UK scores 11 points over the

final 20 minutes—and loses to the Hoyas, 53-40. ... **Turpin** scores an SEC Tournament-record 42 points against Georgia. ... In their first regular-season meeting with Louisville in more than 60 years, the Wildcats hammer the Cardinals, 65-44, at Rupp Arena.

1984-85

18-13. Kentucky drops four of its first five games but regroups to win an NCAA Tournament bid. After beating Washington and UNLV in the tourney, the Cats lose to St. John's in the West Regional semifinals. ... Walker scores 22.9 points per game. ... Hall retires after the end of the season.

1985-86

32-4. **Eddie Sutton** (below) leaves Arkansas to become UK's new coach. ... Walker is a consensus All-American. He also is SEC Player of the Year for the second consecutive season. ... Walker makes all 11 of his field-goal attempts and scores 32 points in an NCAA Tournament win over Western Kentucky. ... Roger Harden averages a UK-record 6.4 assists. ... The season ends with a 59-57 loss to LSU in the NCAA Southeast Regional final.

1986-87

18-11. Freshman sensation Rex Chapman scores 26 points as Kentucky crushes Louisville, 85-51, at Freedom Hall. ... More than 19,000 UK fans attend a Wildcats practice in Louisville. ... The Cats finish 10-8 in the SEC. ... UK again is ousted from the NCAA tourney by Ohio State.

1987-88

25-5. Kentucky loses to Villanova in the NCAA Southeast Regional semifinals. ... The Cats' 2-1 record in the '88 tourney is later stricken from the record because of sanctions imposed by the NCAA.

1988-89

13-19. UK loses a school-record six consecutive SEC games. ... In May, the NCAA places Kentucky on probation for three years because of recruiting and academic violations. The penalty includes a two-year ban from postseason competition.

1989-90

14-14. Rick Pitino, coach of the New York Knicks for two seasons, succeeds Sutton as Kentucky coach. ... In Pitino's fifth game, UK absorbs a 150-95 pounding at Kansas. ... In a season brightener, the Wildcats upset an LSU team featuring Shaquille O'Neal and Chris Jackson. The 100-95 win comes on Feb. 15 at Rupp Arena. ... "Pitino's Bombinos" put up 810 3-point shots and make 281 (99 by **Derrick Miller**).

1990-91

22-6. The Cats post an SEC-best 14-4 record but aren't eligible for the regular-season title because of NCAA sanctions. ... Bernadette Locke joins Pitino's coaching staff after five years as an assistant for the Georgia women's team. Her hiring is considered a gender milestone in Division I men's basketball.

1991-92

29-7. Banned from postseason play the previous two years, Kentucky returns to the spotlight with a stunning season that ends one victory shy of the Final Four. With a nucleus of players who persevered through the probationary years, the Wildcats capture the SEC East crown, win the SEC Tournament and prevail in three NCAA tourney games before losing to Duke—on **Christian Laettner's** overtime jump shot—in the East Regional final. ... The "Laettner game" marks the end of Ledford's career as the voice of the Cats.

1992-93

30-4 Kentucky reaches the Final Four but loses to Michigan in overtime in the semifinals. The Cats dispose of earlier NCAA tourney opponents by margins of 44, 21, 34 and 25 points. ... UK's Jamal Mashburn is a consensus All-American. ... Travis Ford sinks a school-record 101 3-point field goals.

1993-94

27-7. Trailing at LSU by a score of 68-37 with 15:34 to play, the Wildcats outscore the Tigers, 62-27, the rest of the way and pull out an improbable 99-95 victory.

1994-95

28-5. Kentucky is defeated by North Carolina in the Southeast Regional final.

1995-96

34-2. UK wins the NCAA championship with a 76-67 triumph over Syracuse. ... The Wildcats win 27 consecutive games, a single-season Kentucky record. ... **Tony Delk** is a consensus All-American. ... Massachusetts (second game of the season) and Mississippi State (SEC Tournament title game) account for UK's only losses. The Cats get revenge on UMass, beating the Minutemen in the national semifinals. ... The Cats post the SEC's first perfect record in 40 years, going 16-0.

1996-97

35-5. A knee injury ends Derek Anderson's season in mid-January. Anderson is averaging 17.7 points. ... UK shows resilience after losing Anderson, wins 11 of its next 12 games and goes on to cop the SEC Tournament title. ... The Cats reach the NCAA

title game with West Regional victories over Montana, Iowa, St. Joseph's and Utah and a Final Four triumph over Minnesota. But Kentucky fails in its bid for back-to-back national titles, losing to Arizona in overtime. ... North Carolina coach Dean Smith wins his 877th game, passes Rupp as the winningest Division I coach of all time. ... Kentucky's Ron Mercer is a consensus All-American. ... In May, Pitino is named coach of the Boston Celtics. Georgia coach **Orlando "Tubby" Smith**, a former UK assistant, replaces Pitino at Kentucky.

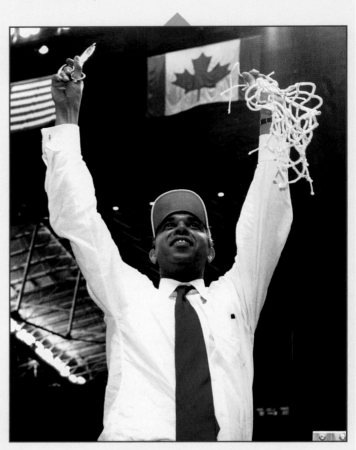

1997-98

35-4. Kentucky wins the NCAA championship. The Wildcats score come-from-behind victories over Duke (South Regional final), Stanford (national semifinals) and Utah (championship game) and claim their seventh national crown. ... The Final Four appearance is Kentucky's 13th. ... After losing to Mississippi on Feb. 14 at Rupp Arena, the Cats run the table. Particularly sweet in the 13-0 finish to the season is the NCAA tourney win over Duke. It comes in the teams' first meeting since the Blue Devils' Christian Laettner broke Kentuckians' hearts in the 1992 East Regional final. ... Jeff Sheppard is the top scorer for the national champs with a 13.7 average, the lowest figure for UK's leading scorer in 50 years. ... Smith's Cats finish 14-2 in the SEC.

Wayne Turner was a big factor in Kentucky's come-from-behind triumph over Duke in the 1998 South Regional final. The guard from Boston, tightly defended on this play by the Blue Devils' Steve Wojciechowski, was the Cats' No. 2 scorer with 16 points and finished with a game-high eight assists.

scores 12.6 points per game. ... After four losses in the final seven regular-season games, the Cats rebound to win the SEC Tournament title.

1999-00

23-10. The Cats are one-and-out in the SEC Tournament and two-and-out in the NCAA tourney. UK loses to Arkansas in the SEC tourney and falls to Syracuse in a second-round NCAA game after beating St. Bonaventure in double overtime. ... Kentucky is only 4-4 after eight games. ... A 76-46 pummeling of Louisville is a highlight of the season.

2000-01

24-10. Kentucky wins or shares the SEC title for the 41st time. ... The Cats dismantle Ole Miss, 77-55, in the SEC Tournament title game. ... The season ends in the NCAA East Regional semifinals, with Southern California bolting to a 31-10 lead over Kentucky and hanging on for an 80-76 victory. ... UK's **Tayshaun Prince** (right) is the SEC's Player of the Year.

2001-02

22-10. UK plays its 99th season of intercollegiate basketball. ... The third consecutive double-figure loss total is a first in school history. ... The UK-Louisville game at Rupp Arena pits the Wildcats against former coach Rick Pitino, who is in his first season as Cardinals coach. Kentucky leads Louisville by four points at halftime, then races to an 82-62 victory. ... The Wildcats lose three games in overtime. ... Prince scores 41 points in UK's 87-82 win over Tulsa in a second-round NCAA Tournament game. The Cats bow out of the tourney in the East Regional semifinals, losing to eventual national champion Maryland.

1998-99

28-9. UK reaches the NCAA Midwest Regional final, loses to Michigan State. ... **Scott Padgett** (above) leads the team in scoring with an average even lower than Sheppard's 1997-98 mark. He

Tayshaun Prince torched Tulsa for 41 points in the 2002 NCAA Tournament.